HeartBeats

the rhythm of love

Gale Alvarez

WESTBOW
PRESS®
A DIVISION OF THOMAS NELSON
& ZONDERVAN

Scripture quotations marked (KJV) are from the King James Version Bible

Scripture quotations marked (ESV) are from the ESV° Bible (The Holy Bible,
English Standard Version°), copyright © 2001 by Crossway, a publishing
ministry of Good News Publishers. Used by permission. All rights reserved.

Scripture Quotations marked (NIV) are from THE HOLY BIBLE, NEW
INTERNATIONAL VERSION°, NIV° Copyright © 1973, 1978, 1984,
2011 by Biblica, Inc.° Used by permission. All rights reserved worldwide.

Scripture quotations marked (NASB) are from Scripture quotations
taken from the New American Standard Bible°, Copyright © 1960,
1962, 1963, 1968, 1971, 1972, 1973, 1975, 1977, 1995 by The Lockman
Foundation Used by permission." (www.Lockman.org)

Scripture quotations marked (NLT) are taken from the Holy Bible,
New Living Translation, copyright © 1996, 2004, 2007 by Tyndale
House Foundation. Used by permission of Tyndale House Publishers,
Inc., Carol Stream, Illinois 60188. All rights reserved.

WestBow Press books may be ordered through booksellers or by contacting:

WestBow Press
A Division of Thomas Nelson & Zondervan
1663 Liberty Drive
Bloomington, IN 47403
www.westbowpress.com
1 (866) 928-1240

Because of the dynamic nature of the Internet, any web addresses or links contained in
this book may have changed since publication and may no longer be valid. The views
expressed in this work are solely those of the author and do not necessarily reflect the
views of the publisher, and the publisher hereby disclaims any responsibility for them.

Any people depicted in stock imagery provided by Thinkstock are models,
and such images are being used for illustrative purposes only.
Certain stock imagery © Thinkstock.

ISBN: 978-1-5127-1665-8 (sc)
ISBN: 978-1-5127-1666-5 (e)

Library of Congress Control Number: 2015917173

Print information available on the last page.

WestBow Press rev. date: 12/08/2015

To My Husband, Jason,

I would not be who I am today without you, for you have truly challenged me to the core in every area of life. We have shared the bitter and the sweet, and we have learned and continue to learn from both. Only God could have known, when we stood at the altar on June 29, 1972, the plan He had for us and what our journey together in the earth would look like. I am so thankful that all the roads have drawn us closer to Him and truly He has made all things beautiful in His time. Thank you, J, for sharing this journey with me. I pray that I make you proud and that you always know my heartbeat is one that longs for you to be all that He has called you to be. You are a gift from God and I am forever grateful.

Dedication

I dedicate *HeartBeats* to Mary Ann Brown, who came into my life as a mother in Israel; and when her love took me in, everything changed. She showed me the power of acceptance, and her example in all things was truly life changing. I wrote her many cards, and after she died of cancer, I received a gift of many of those cards sent back to me with her thoughts on the cards. I was also given one of her Bibles and one of her journals. One day, while reading her journal, I saw that she had hand written portions of my writings into them. I wept knowing how deeply she believed in me and how many hours she spent praying for me. I miss her greatly and I will miss her until I see her again. Thank you, Momma Brown.

Your legacy lives on!

A Dedication To The Future

As I think on the fond memories of my mentor Mary Ann Brown and cherish the many seeds she has planted in my life and the life of others, my thoughts turn to my grandchildren as a hopeful bridge to the future.

I dedicate *HeartBeats* also to my grandchildren Joshua Caleb, Lyla Grace and Liana Marie. Each of you brings me abundant joy and I am thrilled beyond measure to watch you grow, bloom and blossom in the Lord. Sharing life with you is a gift beyond measure and I know He has called you as holy seeds to accomplish good works in the kingdom of God. Abuela loves you and I will never cease to pray for you. I love you with all my heart!

Endorsements

I have never known another woman quite like my wife, Gale. She is divinely unique and remarkably gracious. Her garments drip with love, and her selflessness never wavers. There's none like her, and there is none better!

Pastor Jason Alvarez, Pastor and Founder of the Love of Jesus Family Church and Ministries

Author Gale Alvarez brings inspirational words to life with truth, honesty, and passion. She pours out of her very being and her life experience to engage people where they live. It's so true that people most remember how you make them feel. Gale Alvarez's devotional, *HeartBeats* makes readers come away feeling validated, inspired, and hopeful for a better future and a life worth living.

Valerie J. Fullilove, writer/producer
Trinity Park Productions

I've known Pastor Gale Alvarez for over twenty-seven years, and there has never been a time I have spoken with her that she didn't speak directly to my heart. She is truly a woman of God, filled with wisdom, love, and understanding. This book will graciously impart God's love, wisdom, and mercy to many lives as Pastor Gale has many times blessed my life and the lives of my family. We are thankful for her compassion, commitment, and dedication to the people of God.

Pastor Barbara Glanton
The Love of Jesus Family Church, Newark, New Jersey

My friend Gale Alvarez has been blessed with a special ability to discern the needs of others, the gift of showing love and compassion to those who are broken, and a unique way to articulate the word of healing. As Mary's alabaster box was broken so the ointment could be a blessing to Jesus, and as the fragrance filled the room and enriched those who were present, so the healing ointment that comes of Gale's special journey is a sweet savor to God and will be a blessing to you!

Dr. Gerald G. Loyd
Fountain of Life International Fellowship

After reading this inspiring book, I see life through the eyes and life of a person who has great wisdom. Wisdom can be defined as seeing life and situations from all sides and knowing what to do and what to say and how to respond to every life situation and challenge. The insights in this book help us have a true definition of life and the many winding journeys we may encounter on our journey. Pastor Gale Alvarez has brilliantly described, in such captivating and inspiring depictions, the proper and wise decisions that should be made in many common but often trying situations. This is such a wise and thought-provoking book from a woman who puts her actions where her intentions are—just amazing.

Pastor/Founder, Cassiaus Farrell
The Love of Jesus Family Church, Patterson, New Jersey

Pastor Gale is a visionary with integrity and sterling character. From her gentle elegance but firm, confident voice flow volumes of wisdom. She is a pace setter, contemporary enough to grasp the issues of today, yet traditional enough, by priority, to maintain principles and values of excellence.

Bettye Blackston
Director, the Women of Purpose Ministry

To know Gale Alvarez closely for over three decades has been an honor because in an ever-changing world where devastation and depravity are mounting in our culture, we need the voices from the desert who point us to Christ, the author and finisher of our faith and lives.

HeartBeats is a vulnerable, candid look into the soul of a woman who said, "Yes, Lord, I believe, and now my life belongs to You." Despite profound personal losses, piercing disappointments, and seasons where she walked alone with only the hand of God to cling to, Gale pens simple and yet profound reflections that serve as daily reminders to the steadfast faithfulness of a loving heavenly Father and the passion of His Son for them that believe and call upon His name.

Thank you for displaying the beauty He can make from the ashes of our lives. Thank you for being an example of a living sacrifice. Thank you for being authentic in your life of faith and commitment to Christ and for allowing the Holy Spirit to establish your roots so deeply that we can glean from the fruit of your life and truly understand what it means *in Jeremiah 17:8 (KJV): "For he shall be as a tree planted by the waters, and that spreadeth out her roots by the river, and shall not see when heat cometh, but her leaf shall be green; and shall not be careful in the year of drought, neither shall cease from yielding fruit."*

HeartBeats presents timeless biblical truth, presented to the reader for encouragement in the pursuit of living a victorious life. Gale weaves the wisdom of God's Word with a spirit of counsel that will draw you to a more intimate relationship with the one who breathes life into each heartbeat you have.

Dawn Chillon, MA theology, PhD psychology
Founder, the Foundation Family of Healing

I have known Gale Alvarez for over thirty years through ministry and close friendship. Within this time frame I have seen the unveiling of a heart full of passion and longing to commune with the Father. Gale has developed an addiction to His presence. If you sit more than two minutes with her you will hear the heartbeat of God through her words of wisdom. She has the ability to not only seek but also find Him in any situation, whether good or bad, and exhibit an even greater gift of revealing Him to others. Her writings reflect the countless hours of practicing His presence and desiring that we all see Him and cling to Him through every circumstance. This book will be a necessary and very timely read for all!

Reverend Pat Higgins
Restoration Family Church, Hillside, New Jersey

Gale Alvarez's passionate reflections from *HeartBeats* are truly pearls of great price. Gale's approach is so refreshing one cannot read a line fast enough to get to the next line. It is evident that Gale has taken the circumstances that life has served her as opportunities to find God and ever press into a greater love and knowledge of the Most High!

Above all, it's easy to see upon whose chest her head has been resting and whose heartbeats have enthralled her into exciting revelations of how to encounter God on a daily basis. Anyone who reads this will want to keep Gale's thoughts very close to their hearts. *Enjoy*!

Prophet Barry E. Taylor
Founder, Liberty Ministries Inc.

Contents

Foreword

After doing some research on what goes into a Foreword, I realized it was a special place in the book where the reader is introduced to the author and their literary work by someone other than the author. As I searched for truthful words to bring impact upon a reader, I instantly realized that the words for the Foreword were already etched in the hearts of those who were touched in deep ways by Gale Alvarez's inspired ***HeartBeats***.

Here are those heart felt words and hence the Foreword:

- This is such a breath of fresh air.
- Your voice is a voice of kindness.
- I need to write that on the inside of my eyelids.
- You're like a breath mint … so refreshing!
- I can't tell you how many times in my darkness and desperate hours, your words encouraged me.
- Your words are so powerful. They're not just words; they are life.
- We need you and the honest anointing that comes with and from you.
- This is truth, amazing words of wisdom.
- Very profound, from a seasoned woman of God.
- I needed to hear this word.
- It builds, it beautifies, it buffs—wonderful …
- I appreciate "check yourself moments" all to be closer to Him, to please Him, and to build up one another.

- What a beautiful love story.
- Your words are always a blessing.
- I will follow your admonition not to give up.
- You seriously need to be behind a pulpit regularly with the wisdom God pouring through you. Seriously!
- So precious. Thank you for the reminder, Gale.
- Gale, you are a wise soul.

I say to the LORD, "You are my Lord; apart from you I have no good thing." (Psalm 16:2 NIV)

Julio Vitolo

Introduction
My Heart Beats For Him And It Beats For You

This is a book of my *HeartBeats* that started out with simple messages to help encourage myself and my friends in their daily journey. Each day as I wrote what was on my heart, I could sense the beat of my own heart praying for the hearts of others who believed their hearts could or would never beat again. As I sensed the impossible situations my friends were facing, I was driven to share the unlimited possibilities of a loving, merciful God, and hence, *HeartBeats* was born.

I have been in lifeless situations and deeply understand the feeling of hopelessness that can settle down on the inside of us. Sometimes the darkness can settle in so deep that we feel like we have no beat left in us, no air to breathe. As I wrote my simple messages, I became amazed at what a word can do to change someone's perspective or how a loving thought can flip the switch on the inside to cause a song to suddenly come alive in a broken heart. Where there once was no beat, no song, no hope, just shattered pieces, now a sweet melody arises. *HeartBeats* are words sent to me that have changed my life and the lives of others. We all have a song, we all have a *HeartBeat*; we just have to find it.

I lived many a year as a dead woman walking until I met the Creator who makes all things beautiful in His time. When I learned of His love and allowed Him to take me in, everything changed. He told me of His everlasting love. He drew me with loving kindness and made me aware of how wonderful we are in His eyes. Thankfully I am far from perfect. I still go through hard times, but now He is the difference. I know where to run to, how to get there, and most importantly, who to run to.

I suffered much excruciating loss from an early age, and that loss left a hole so deep in me that it shattered my being into a mess of broken, tearful, painful pieces. Have you ever noticed that if we drop something that shatters into many pieces, we don't even try to piece it all back together again but rather tend to sweep up the broken pieces and just throw them away? Yet if we drop something—let's say a dish—and only a few pieces break off we gather the pieces, glue them back together, and position the dish back on the shelf in such a way so that no one ever knows it was even broken. I am so thankful that God can take every shattered piece of our lives and make it whole again. He restores, and His warranty never runs out. As a matter of fact, His love never runs out. He makes us new all over again so that we can live life as a brand new creation made in His glorious Image.

My *HeartBeats* are a gift to me and yours to keep. These HeartBeats contain tears, joy, laughter, hope, grace, and mostly His love and promise to you and me for a better life and eternal one with *Him*.

In this *HeartBeats* collection you will read of the bitter and the sweet, the hard times and the easy, breezy times where the sun is shining and you think it will never rain again. I know now, more than ever, that it will rain again, but now I can rein in the rain and find refuge from the storm.

My heart ached for such a long time, and there was such a need for an expression to go out from me that I started writing simple, honest thoughts about where I was in the midst of it all. I didn't realize there would be such a sacred, overwhelming response from those who were also going through it, searching for a word in season that would bring relief from the same pain I was feeling, for a *HeartBeat* that would restore newness of life,

Many of you have asked me to put my messages in a book, so with your inspiration, I have done just that; I've created *HeartBeats*, hopefully the first of many, with you in mind. I sense the beating of His heart and the beating of my heart that desires to take you to a place within yourself where you once again will find life's rhythm.

It's truly my deep, sincere hope that within these pages you will find a refreshing, a refueling, and a rhythm that beats with passion to live with grace in the fullness of His new life. Trust the Lord, for He will lead you deeper, closer, and higher than you ever thought possible.

I love you,
Gale Alvarez

Now unto him that is able to do exceeding abundantly above all that we ask or think, according to the power that worketh in us, Unto him be glory in the church by Christ Jesus throughout all ages, world without end. Amen. (Ephesians 3:20–21 KJV)

Many waters cannot quench love, neither can the floods drown it. (Song of Solomon 8:7 KJV)

Am I Being Kind Enough?

Every day I am amazed at what He does and who He uses to be an extension of Himself. Life's journey brings us across the path of many, and as we reach out to others, it is wise to be conscious of how we would want to be treated and remembered. I often catch myself as I react with others thinking, *Is this how I want to be treated?* Then I become very attentive as I say to myself, *Is this how I want God to treat me?* That is a sobering thought and constant guide as we relate to others. *"Do to others as you would have them do to you" (Luke 6:31 NIV).*

Are we listening? Are we rushing? Are we really concerned? I sat with a young man today who thanked me for speaking into his life years ago. When I got home, I realized that some things he had said to me were speaking into my life. It was pleasant to know that God kept *His* Word in that I was able to reap some kindness I had sown many years ago. I pray we will always be ready to be Christ to someone, always ready to love someone, always ready to lift one another in the hope of God, and always ready to encourage one another in the grace of God, to become more like *Him*.

Be devoted to one another in love. Honor one another above yourselves. (Romans 12:10 NIV)

He Restores My Soul

I cherished every moment away and am thankful that I left behind what I needed to in order to receive all He had for me while I was away. Learning the lesson of unpacking my mind with stuff I should not take when He creates a space for us to embrace renewal is one of the greatest lessons I've ever learned.

The apostle Paul left his former life behind and didn't look back when God created the greatest renewal imaginable—a new space for him in Christ. The apostle's famous words were, *"What is more, I consider everything a loss because of the surpassing worth of knowing Christ Jesus my Lord" (Philippians 3:8 NASB).*

Yes, going away provided rest and renewal and I so appreciate that time, but going away reminded me of the greater renewal: the renewal of leaving it all behind to gain Christ. Let us also leave it all behind and say,

He makes me lie down in green pastures; He leads me beside quiet waters. He restores my soul; He guides me in the paths of righteousness For His name's sake. (Psalm 23:2–3 NASB)

Restore us to You, O LORD, that we may be restored; Renew our days as of old. (Lamentations 5:21 NASB)

Lord, Make My Heart Beat

I will never forget the day He gave me a new wineskin for my heart. Where I was empty, He filled me with new wine, new love, new hope, new energy, and new conviction. Each day I am grateful for that day, and yet maintaining it is not always easy. Sometimes I drift, sometimes I am pulled into other dimensions, and sometimes I am torn, but He always draws me back, close to *Him*.

Closer, closer, closer, the closer I get to Him and the more I see from His perspective, the more the rhythm of my heart aligns with His. My beat gets stronger, louder, purer, beating with electric energy that only He provides. My life becomes radiant, joyful, hopeful, beating with eternal beats that bring life not only to me but they also press hard into the hearts of others as they have lost their beat but now find *His*. Father, You are my heart cry, my heartbeat, my heart song. Beat in me, Lord, so through me You may beat in others.

My soul thirsts for God, for the living God.
(Psalm 42:2 NASB)

A new heart also will I give you, and a new spirit will I put within you: and I will take away the stony heart out of your flesh, and I will give you an heart of flesh.
(Ezekiel 36:26 KJV)

Steal A Dream Or Make One Happen

It is out of the abundance of the heart that the mouth speaks. Therefore it is vital to protect our hearts and be careful of the things we allow in them. Life's journey can become a maze of emotions when you let issues take over your mind, seep into your heart, and soon after come out of your mouth.

I encourage you today to listen to what is coming out of your mouth and check up on what's living in your heart that needs to be thrown out. Father, *"Let the words of my mouth, and the meditation of my heart, be acceptable in your sight" (Psalm 19:14 ESV)*. With faith-filled words we can move mountains, call things that are not as though they are, still storms, and even proclaim the eternal good news. A harsh word can steal a dream; a good word can make one happen.

The good person out of the good treasure of his heart produces good, and the evil person out of his evil treasure produces evil, for out of the abundance of the heart his mouth speaks. (Luke 6:45 ESV)

A soft answer turneth away wrath: but grievous words stir up anger. (Proverbs 15:1 KJV)

Love Bait

When it was time to go, I felt the weight of leaving and had to come to terms with the fact that my dear friend, the one who had taught me so much, the one who had influenced me to the core, was really no longer in the earth. As I walked around her house, and later walked in my house, I saw gifts we gave each other, photos of times shared together, and notes of expression that we sent each other. These are memories I will forever hold dear.

It is important to cherish the moments in our lives and know that our times are in His hands. We are His, and He never fails us. We are important because He is important. Our moments are important because He is in them and we are privileged to share Him in every thing we do. When you say good morning, smile to a cashier in the supermarket, or say thank you to your postman, do all you do knowing He is in your actions ready to reach out to a lonely soul who needs the love you have inside. We are people changers because He made us fishers of men and woman. We are His fishing rods, and the bait is His overwhelming, unfailing love. Saints, freely we have received so freely give. There is eternity in your giving.

Love is patient, love is kind. (1 Corinthians 13:4 NIV)

Be Love

The older I get, the more I understand the statement, "When someone shows you who they are, believe them." The understanding of that did not come easy to me but I get it now. I must own my truth and live it out loud, and at the same time when someone shows or tells me their truth, I must see it, accept it, and go on living.

God's Word clearly teaches me what love is, and in that I also get a clear glimpse of what love is not. Thank You, Father, for being love personified. I pray that each one of us will stop looking for love in all the wrong places or seeking love from someone who is not in passionate pursuit of relationship with us the way He is. He is what love looks like, He is what love is, and He is love. Be love and You will find love; He is love.

There is no greater love than to lay down one's life for one's friends. (John 15:13 NLT)

We love him, because he first loved us. (1 John 4:19 KJV)

Make Your Way, My Way

When I made the decision to follow Him all my days, I understood that I would always be behind Him and never in front of Him. I have never regretted the decision to be a follower, and my heart takes comfort in knowing the one who leads me on. It's so sad that some see themselves as the leader and expect Him to follow, only to find themselves in an isolated place by doing their own thing. Doing your own thing sounds good, but if your own thing is not His thing, it will lead nowhere and cost you dearly.

Check in with the Lord; He will guide you. I pray that each of us will stay in our lane, maintain our position, be willing to be guided, and always know Him who leads us in truth, into truth and life.

Shew me thy ways, O LORD; teach me thy paths. Lead me in thy truth, and teach me: for thou art the God of my salvation; on thee do I wait all the day. (Psalm 25:4–5 KJV)

Thus says the LORD, your Redeemer, the Holy One of Israel, "I am the LORD your God, who teaches you to profit, Who leads you in the way you should go." (Isaiah 48:17 NASB)

He Keeps Bringing It

I remember a time in my life when I used to sing, "Rainy days and Mondays always get me down." Then I met Him. I no longer sing sad songs, and I absolutely love rainy days. It is clear to me that He is my sunshine and His light brings life and lifts us wherever we are when we look to Him.

God brings me joy. He brings me hope. He brings me everything I need in this life and the life to come. He brings me consolation, laughter, and rest; He brings me grace sufficient, resolve, and the peace of God that surpasses all understanding. He brings me love. He brings me courage. He brings me the evidence of things not seen. He brings the sunshine; He is my sunshine and the lifter of my head. He just keeps on bringing it day after day. Yes, He brings me to Himself.

"He who rules over men righteously, Who rules in the fear of God, Is as the light of the morning when the sun rises, A morning without clouds, When the tender grass springs out of the earth, Through sunshine after rain."
(2 Samuel 23:24 NASB)

On Course

Not every day goes the way we plan it, and that's not a bad thing. Actually, things not going our way could be a blessing as we recognize the one who is planning our way. Some of the greatest blessings come when we take our hands off the wheel and allow the one and only loving God to do the steering.

Doesn't He lead us beside still waters? Doesn't He draw us to Himself? Doesn't He always lead us along paths that have been ordained for fulfillment? Doesn't He lead the way to joy? Doesn't He lead us in paths of truth? Doesn't He lead us by peace, into peace? When we choose to live completely surrendered, sold out and singled out to Him, and trust He is directing our steps, we can live each day knowing we are on course—His course, the course to abundant life. He is the good Shepherd, and we shall not want.

You make known to me the path of life; in your presence there is fullness of joy; at your right hand are pleasures forevermore. (Psalm 16:11 ESV)

Change Has Many Faces

Looking out my window, I see change in many ways. I see leaves changing into an array of brilliant, glorious colors, and yet at the same time I see the result of trees that have let go of their leaves. Now they stand with no luster, barren. I am reminded that there are times when it is easy and colorful to let go and then there are times when we hold on a little too long in the process of change.

I so desire to be the one who listens and knows the when, why, where, what, and how of life. When I ask, He answers; I find these answers in His Word. Life's journey with its changing seasons is not always easy. The process can be weary at times, yet as we yield, stay close, and daily surrender to Him, we will begin to understand that obedience is always better than sacrifice. Today my heart sings, *"Create in me a clean heart, O God" (Psalm 51:10 KJV)*. Yes I sing with a joyful heart, for I am His.

But we all, with open face beholding as in a glass the glory of the Lord, are changed into the same image from glory to glory, even as by the Spirit of the Lord.
(2 Corinthians 3:1 KJV)

Which Way Is Up?

When you seek Him you will find Him, and that's a promise from Him. If you find yourself walking around in a circle not able to find who or what you are looking for, then I believe it's time to take a break and consider who and what you are seeking after.

My greatest desire in life is to know Him, hear Him, and follow after Him, for He is life to me and without Him I am nothing. I was created for His purpose, and without Him life has no meaning. It really is all about Him, and all to Him I freely give.

My sheep hear my voice, and I know them, and they follow me. (John 10:27 KJV)

For where your treasure is, there will your heart be also. (Matthew 6:21KJV)

You will seek me and find me, when you seek me with all your heart. (Jeremiah 29:13 ESV)

You Are Everything To Me

Palm Beach weather is absolutely gorgeous. It felt so good to be away, and I am so grateful that He created a space and a place for a needed time. It takes discipline to leave the cares of home behind and not allow them to invade a time of refreshing and reflection.

Father, I thank You that You can keep that which we commit unto You, and I pray that each one of us will have grace to commit the whole of our cares to You, knowing You care for us. We trust in Your provision, Lord; You know our every need, our every step, our every breath, our every aspiration. We thank You, Father, for times of refreshing and for Your faithful promises that always provide everything and anything we need in ways that are far more than all we can think, ask, or imagine.

Lord, you are the giver of all good gifts; you leave us wanting nothing. You grant us peace and grace that is sufficient. Thank You, Lord, for all that You are, for Your love that lifts us, for Your hope that sustains us, for Your essence that feeds us daily. Thank You, Lord, for filling our hearts with joy unspeakable; Lord, You are everything to me, everything to us.

I say to the LORD, "You are my Lord; apart from you I have no good thing." (Psalm 16:2 NIV)

On Which Road Do You Travel?

Some of us travel the road less traveled while others find themselves on busy streets or stuck in traffic in their journey. Regardless where you might find yourself, it is vital to make the time and the space to spend some time with Him. Even if you don't have a red light, Stop and Listen. I am sure He has something of worth to say to you, something good, something that will bring you to your destination, with ease and with His comfort. Come apart before you come apart. Give Him your ear and your attention; He has a green light and an open door for you to enter.

Life is real and sometimes unfair; we often don't see what's coming, but He does. Life's challenges can press and overwhelm our days; they can shift our direction, interfere with our nights and leave us sleepless, hopeless and helpless. I encourage you not to allow the street you find yourself on to determine your relationship with Him. Instead, look to Him, walk with Him, talk to Him, trust Him and believe on Him. He will surely be your guide and grant you the energy, wisdom and grace to accomplish your plans as you surrender them to Him.

As they were going along the road, someone said to him, "I will follow you wherever you go." (Luke 9:57 ESV)

The LORD directs the steps of the godly. He delights in every detail of their lives. (Psalm 37:23 NLT)

'Call unto me, and I will answer thee, and shew thee great and mighty things, which thou knowest not.' (Jeremiah 33:3 KJV)

A voice is calling, "Clear the way for the LORD in the wilderness; Make smooth in the desert a highway for our God." (Isaiah 40:3)

Impossible Is Possible For God

Today I find myself joyfully declaring life over you. Sometimes we allow setbacks in our journey to knock the wind out of us, leaving us gasping for air and fighting for life. God wants to breathe life into you again. He wants to restore all that has been stolen from you and He longs for you to believe He is willing and able to set your feet 'a dancing' with a new song in your heart; a song that declares victory, new life, joy, and hope for a future. Don't faint, don't give in to the pressure, don't give up and whatever you do, don't take situations into your own hands. Wait on the Lord, put your total trust in Him, commit your plans to Him; give Him your burdens, give Him your battles, surrender your struggle and you will see the deliverance of the Lord. Look to Him and know that this situation is not unto death but rather for the glory of God. When you give Him the impossible, he will bring you the possible.

But Jesus looked at them and said, "With man this is impossible, but with God all things are possible."
(Matthew 19:26 ESV)

Don't Fall For Old Traps

There are things that happen in life's journey that cause us to get to a place of questioning Him. From the very beginning of time, the Enemy has desired to move us from faith to doubt and then to fear by planting thoughts that put us in a position where we are asking, "Has God really said that?" We must recognize that the Enemy has no new tricks and really does not need any because many keep falling for the old traps.

Encourage yourself in the Lord today. Stay faithful, faith filled, and full of purpose, promise, and passion. Just keep reminding yourself, God says yes to your fulfillment, yes to your joy, yes to who you are in Him, and be convinced that His Word does not ever return void.

And Jesus answered and said unto them, Take heed that no man deceive you. For many shall come in my name, saying, I am Christ; and shall deceive many. (Matthew 24:4–5 KJV)

The thief comes only to steal and kill and destroy. I came that they may have life and have it abundantly. (John 10:10 ESV)

What's With You?

Some days are encouraging while other days are filled with discouragement, disappointment, and details that need not be spoken. Instead, let us speak of His love, His greatness, and His ability to change circumstances rather than speak of the despair we think we face, but truly we don't. There is no despair in God, no fear, no doubt, no disappointment. With God all things are possible.

In all of life's experiences, I find Him to be my sufficiency as I learn to continually draw from His wells of salvation, from His wells of enduring hope. If He holds eternal life, how much more does He hold us in His hands? He makes old things new. He calms all storms, and He makes a way where there is no way. Yes, He is the great way maker, the life changer, the love giver. He speaks and it is finished; He decrees and it is accomplished. There is no doubt between His thought and His creation. He said, "Let light be," and light was. There is no feeling that He is not touched by or any infirmity He cannot heal. When emotions run high, they can cause me to look down rather than up, and in those times I remind myself that He upholds all things and that includes me. I love you.

Behold, God is my helper; The Lord is the sustainer of my soul. (Psalm 54:4 NASB)

Listen For Those Gentle Whispers

As I waited for my daughter to come home from the prom last night, I thought of how quickly the days pass, how precious they are, and how many destinations we stop at in our journey along the way. We meet many people, and we learn from all of them. With some we learn what to do and with others we learn what not to do; yet what remains important is that we learn and increase in our capacity to be loved by Him, to love Him and to love others.

I cared for and carried many things and people in my life's journey that perhaps I should have laid aside earlier than I did but I thought I could help. Unfortunately all help offered is not always help received or perceived the way it is given. Ultimately I believe if we give with pure intentions, God will keep us from harm in situations we should not have been in, and He promises to use all things for our good. Yet we should get wisdom, for wisdom is supreme. We should *"cry aloud for understanding and look for it as for hidden treasure, then you will understand the fear of the Lord and find the knowledge of God" (Proverbs 2:3–5 NIV).* May we all seek to hear His voice as a priority, for when we do, be assured, He will lead us by abundant, still waters.

And after the fire there was the sound of a gentle whisper. (1 Kings 19:12 NLT)

It's All About Him,
And He's All About Us

When you're up all night caring for someone, it makes you even more grateful that He never sleeps or slumbers. It is a truth that I know, but when I am in the thick of things, it takes on a deeper level and He settles my heart. We are truly so blessed to know Him. He is the one who is forever interceding for us, calling our names, directing our paths, supplying our needs, providing grace, granting mercy, equipping us for battle, giving good gifts, renewing our minds, lighting our paths, ordering our steps, giving us peace, increasing our knowledge, drawing us closer, quenching our thirst, and giving us good sleep, the rest we need.

He never sleeps, He never slumbers, and even though it's all about *Him*, He is all about us!

My help comes from the LORD, who made heaven and earth. He will not let your foot be moved; he who keeps you will not slumber. Behold, he who keeps Israel will neither slumber nor sleep. The LORD is your keeper; the LORD is your shade on your right hand. (Psalm 121:2–5 ESV)

Spring Is Coming
(Your Winter Is Over)

I am always glad when winter is over. The frigid cold turns to a reassuring warmth, and the snow becomes lush green grass. Although winter has its reasons, when I'm in it, I really do miss the warmth and the newness of spring. I get excited knowing that flowers will bloom again, sweet fragrances will fill the air, and luxurious colors will be what I will see again on my daily walks. Winters can be hard. Sometimes our seasons are like that, but we endure them and go on.

I encourage you not to cave into depression or sadness but be encouraged that your spring is coming and new growth is happening. Even though we may not see it with our eyes, our inner sense tells us more joy is coming. May you sense new growth inside of you even in a barren season. Embrace His springtime; be fruitful, be hopeful, and multiply joy wherever you go, for as surely as the seasons change, He will make a change for you.

"For I am about to do something new. See, I have already begun! Do you not see it? I will make a pathway through the wilderness. I will create rivers in the dry wasteland"
(Isaiah 43:19 NLT)

There's A Bigger Picture

In the ups and downs of the journey, I see hills and valleys that are both essential parts of life, designed for our good. I have learned to be content in all things, for truly there is great gain in growing in all seasons. Discontentment leads to murmuring and complaining. It leads to attitudes that will diminish growth, work against faith, make things worse, and waste precious time. If you want different results in anything then you must approach things differently, with a positive perspective, with the right attitude, and ultimately with the right action.

If we can see circumstances as gifts sent by God to propel us to our destiny, this view will allow us to embrace obstacles or issues as an opportunity to grow in fullness, to grow in grace. If we keep our eyes on the powerful, glorious potential placed within us, then temporary setbacks or inconveniences will only be temporary experiences that propel us to our purpose. I pray for those going through change; I pray they will see the bigger picture, the wonderful vision for their lives, that they will grasp faith and grace and move through their situations with the sure hope of getting to the other side.

But godliness actually is a means of great gain when accompanied by contentment.
(1 Timothy 6:6–9 NASB)

"For I know the plans I have for you," declares the LORD, "plans to prosper you and not to harm you, plans to give you hope and a future."
(Jeremiah 29:11 NIV)

Relentless Love Reached Me

Trust was always a huge issue in my life; it was something I felt would never change. When you aren't free to trust, you lose out on opportunities meant for you to receive. A lack of trust puts you in a dark world where light is blocked from entering, walls are built, and many who do love you aren't allowed to enter. Sometimes God is also left outside the gates of mistrust, and that is truly sad.

Fortunately, the Lord's stubborn, overwhelming, relentless love pierced my shield of insecurity and made a straight way to my guarded and isolated heart. To this day it still amazes me how much He loved and pursued me, how much He changed my life, and how much my life continues to change because of His care for me. Knowing that the supreme lover of all loves you with a supernatural love changes everything. There are no more walls, no more gates, no more pretenses, but instead open arms, open ears, and an open heart for love to enter and an open heart reaching out to those who are locked up in their own prisons of mistrust.

Mistrust is a lonely world, but love changes all. Disappointments still happen, betrayals will never be easy, and tests, trials, and temptations will continue till the end of our days in the earth. The difference now is the light of *His* love that allows faith to know He is there in the midst of it all and that *His* love never fails. How awesome and almost unimaginable is it that we have Him, the Creator of the universe, to put our trust in. He is the one who will always remain faithful. Now I can sing of His love forever, and forever I will trust Him.

We love, because He first loved us. (1 John 4:19 KJV)

Surely your goodness and unfailing love will pursue me all the days of my life, and I will live in the house of the LORD forever. (Psalm 23:6 NLT)

Settled, Safe, And Secure

I have experienced seasons in my life thinking they would last forever. How often I would have rather quit than endure, but He is faithful. There have been people in my life I was sure would be life-timers, but for some reason or another, they left or we drifted. There is much about the journey I thought was stable, secure, and solid, yet there were times of great instability where natural security was not to be found. Yet when all is said and done, He alone remains the same, stable, and secure. He is my steadfast love. He is the whisper in the wind. He is the great I am, the rock on which I stand, my stability and my peace. I am because He is; He is the beginning and the end.

I pray that we would all become settled in Him, secure on the inside regardless the season, for truly He is the just weight, the measure of our peace. Father, help us to be found faithful, standing in hope, fulfilled in Your presence, with the peace of God you alone can give that surpasses all understanding. Lord, let this be our finest hour as we draw closer to You, as we press on to our high calling in Christ with an ever-increasing love and awareness of You.

For he himself is our peace. (Ephesians 2:14 ESV)

And the peace of God, which passeth all understanding, shall keep your hearts and minds through Christ Jesus. (Philippians 4:7 KJV)

Could Never Have Made It
Without Him

Today I looked at my High School graduation picture sitting on my piano. The image made me think of where I was then and where I am today. The apostle Paul touched on growing up with his remark, *"When I was a child, I spoke and thought and reasoned as a child. But when I grew up, I put away childish things" (1 Corinthians 13:11 NLT).* Life changes, we change, we think differently, we act differently, and we have different priorities. I will always cherish those early years and the many special friends I am still in contact with today.

Life's journey is a blink, and the days pass quickly. God's Word tells us we are like a mist that appears and then disappears. Our lives and time here are a miracle; it's a gift. Therefore I refuse to let a single day pass me by without being ever so grateful for every breath I breathe, for every move I make, for everything He's given. I am especially grateful for His mercy, His grace, His goodness and His love. If there is anything I know with certainty, I surely know I could never have made it without *Him.* He is everything to me.

He is before all things, and in Him all things hold together. (Colossians 1:17 NASB)

Color
My World

I remember the first day of fall, and although I did not see many fallen leaves, I knew they were coming. I am filled with wonder by this time of year. As the leaves begin to change color, I am always inspired by the many vibrant, new colors that appear where there once were uniform green leaves. It's easy to see in my own life how seasonal things have changed me too, and I pray that I will always represent Him with color, for truly He has colored my world.

The Lord will not waste any of your colors, times, or trials. There is a time for every season, and He is faithful to bring meaningful color in every season.

Your eyes have seen my unformed substance; And in Your book were all written The days that were ordained for me, When as yet there was not one of them. (Psalm 139:16 NASB)

And we all, who with unveiled faces contemplate the Lord's glory, are being transformed into his image with ever-increasing glory, which comes from the Lord, who is the Spirit. (2 Corinthians 3:18 NIV)

Seeing Is Not Believing

We must learn to trust Him when we feel like we cannot trace Him. Often I can hear myself say, "Lord, where are You in this? Why is this happening?" The mystery of God is the fact that He is working all things for good regardless of how our circumstances may look.

We may not understand certain outcomes, but one thing is for sure: we can always and forever trust Him. We can trust His love and mercy because He's always perfecting that which concerns us. He may close a door, withhold a certain wish, delay an expectation, end a relationship, open a door, close a door, change your job, or even allow a great disappointment, but everything He does is all for your good. Often He will put up road blocks to mercifully change your direction. His direction is one direction, one way, toward *Him*, away from vanity, away from delusion, away from self, away from destruction, away from anything that is not fruitful, not *Him*.

Feelings are good—they feel good, they make us happy, they make us sad—but we can't trust our feelings; there is only *one* we can trust. We can trust Him. When we live in the perspective that our heavenly Father is working all things for good, we can see life through the lens of *hope*, through the lens of mercy, through the lens of destiny, through the lens of His purposes, knowing that *all is well*. No matter what it looks like, He will work it out. Stand today and declare, "I trust Him, and I shall not be moved. It is well with my soul."

Commit thy way unto the LORD; trust also in him; and he shall bring it to pass. (Psalm 37:5 KJV)

For we live by faith, not by sight. (2 Corinthians 5:7 NIV)

Nothing Shall Separate Us

Many times in the journey we can get lost in the midst of circumstances and find ourselves living in fear rather than faith, in unrest rather than rest. Perhaps we have been overpowered and deceived by a deadly darkness, taken by surprise, or attacked while our guard was down and haven't yet meditated on the love of God that forgives, heals, and washes away all fear. Perfect love casts out all fear and gives us the confidence to cast the whole of our care on *Him*.

When we fall away from the peace and rest of God, we will become overwhelmed with our own efforts and become wastefully focused on things that will deplete our energy and throw us off balance. We must recognize that anything not directed by His purpose cannot live in the same room with *Him*. Be on guard; every day the Enemy seeks to pull us into an arena of doubt, fear, anxiety, and hopelessness, a place where there is no mercy, a place of no grace, a place of condemnation, a place where the love of God is not to be found. Our Lord will always bring us to a place of unfailing love, hope, and perfect peace if we allow ourselves to be led into His presence.

His arms are open wide. His mercy is available, and His grace is abundant. Fear not. Call unto Him, for He is faithful to save you from all failure and harm. Dear Lord, open the eyes of our hearts, enlighten us so we may believe what You say about us rather than giving in to hopeless thoughts not of Your making. I pray that Your people would hunger for Your words of promise so much that they would eat them and be nourished once again. "*Thy words were found, and I did eat them; and thy word was unto me the joy and rejoicing of mine heart: for I am called by thy name, O Lord God of hosts*" (Jeremiah 15:16 KJV). Trust in the Lord. His stubborn love will always draw you, forgive you, and daily shower you with His endless grace. He loves you with an everlasting love.

For I am persuaded, that neither death, nor life, nor angels, nor principalities, nor powers, nor things present, nor things to come, Nor height, nor depth, nor any other creature, shall be able to separate us from the love of God, which is in Christ Jesus our Lord. (Romans 8:38–39 KJV)

What Love Looks Like

When He said, "It is finished," He meant it. I think too many times we try to hold on to people and things in our lives that mean something to us but we have no meaning to them. That's a hard place to live in, especially for those who value relationship, give of themselves without restraint, and sincerely desire to love and be loved.

I am forever grateful for being found by the one I love, by the one who loves me and knew me before I was even formed in the womb. I can now love because He first loved me. When I think of His love toward mankind, of His total rejection, how He stood in silence, with arms opened wide, suffering for us, showing us what love looks like, I am left without words. His love goes beyond expression, beyond anything I can ever imagine. I want to love the way He loves, and I want to know that when my life is finished, I too will have remained with arms wide open, also showing what love looks like. Tonight I sense the pain of loss. In my loss I find Him who found me, and once again I am changed by His love.

Greater love has no one than this, that one lay down his life for his friends. (John 15:13 NASB)

Let the Weak Say I Am Strong

Thank God we know that we have a helper. When it was time for Jesus to go to the Father, He did not leave us helpless. He provided us with a Comforter, a Helper, a Counselor in the person of the Holy Spirit. There are times when we can feel helpless, and I remember one such day of total frailty as I battled a virus that sought to knock me out. I rejoice now and thank God we can look to our Helper, who reminds us of a sure promise that when we are weak, He will make us strong.

The Holy Spirit is our *parakletos*, the one who comes beside us, the one who walks with us through the valley of the shadow of death, the one who brings us close to the Father. The Holy Spirit prays with us, He walks beside us to guide us into all truth, to bring us hope, to help us in our weaknesses. The Lord is trustworthy, and our confidence shall not be shaken. Let the weak say I am strong. Call upon Him; He is with us.

For the sake of Christ, then, I am content with weaknesses, insults, hardships, persecutions, and calamities. For when I am weak, then I am strong. (2 Corinthians 12:10 ESV)

Yea, though I walk through the valley of the shadow of death, I will fear no evil: for thou art with me. (Psalm 23:4 KJV)

Kiss Me

As I think about my Lord today, I weep at what He endured for my sake. Now I see in a deeper level the question He asked in *Luke 22:48 (KJV), "But Jesus said unto him, 'Judas, betrayest thou the Son of man with a kiss?'"* As I mediate on these words, I imagine what His heart of love felt like in that moment. I imagine His grief, His pain, His purpose, and His reality, and tears just stream down my face. I have felt the pain of rejection, betrayal, and the kiss of Judas in my journey, but I did not respond as I see He did; He did not take it personally. He knew what was to come, that it was not only part of the eternal plan for *His* life but as well part of the eternal plan for you and me.

While Jesus was eating with Judas and His disciples, He said in *John 13:27 (KJV), "That thou doest do quickly."* Although Jesus was prepared for *His* destiny, the reality of it was still painful. Yet He endured with joy the suffering that was set before *Him*.

Oh, God, strengthen every weak place in us that we would remain loyal to You, to Your purpose, to the destiny You have called us to. You know the condition of our hearts, and I willingly give You my heart to break and to shape, that I would become like You in accepting with joyful praise any hardship for the sake of You and those You love.

Thank You, Lord, that we need not beg for Your love, Your attention, or Your affirmation, for You give freely and You love freely. You are mine, and I am yours. *Lord, Your kiss is my destiny.* May we stay lovely in the journey and never betray you or anyone else with a Judas kiss.

Looking unto Jesus the author and finisher of our faith; who for the joy that was set before him endured the cross, despising the shame, and is set down at the right hand of the throne of God. (Hebrews 12:2 KJV)

Throw Them Overboard

Every new day begins in darkness yet in this midnight hour I sense hope for relationships. The sun rises, and with it will rise new opportunities, fresh perception, new mercy, and grace. We must never lose sight of our God-given resource, that *"faith is the substance of things hoped for and the evidence of things not yet seen" (Hebrews 11:1 KJV)*. Even in darkness we have His light that shines brighter and brighter through the darkest day, for light will always dispel darkness. May we never allow anyone or anything to hinder us from shining bright as a vessel of His truth.

Our relationship with God is based on the light of God's truth, and so also our relationships with others should be based on His light, on transparency and truth in our inward parts. Father, help us to shine and radiate Your glory at all times. Remove every relationship that causes us to hide or keeps us from growing in the nevertheless life; *"I am crucified with Christ: nevertheless, I live; yet not I but Christ liveth in me. (Galatians 2:20 KJV).* If we cannot walk transparently, open, unashamed, and in respect of one another then the house will fall, and great will be the fall, for a house divided will always fall, and it will never produce fruit that remains. The Lord instructs us not to be unequally yoked. Show us, O God, who the Jonahs are in our lives, the ones who are running, the ones who are not supposed to be there, the ones who keep us from getting where You have destined us to be.

Give us courage, Lord, in your mercy to throw the Jonah overboard to his or her place of grace and repentance so that we and the Jonah can each reach our respective destinies, our places of milk and honey.

Father, I pray let not emotions get in the way of light and lessons needed to be learned. Loyalty to Your Word, not to emotions, will always lead to the obedience that is always better than sacrifice. Lord, may all those who are burdened in emotionally unsafe relationships be set free from those who hinder freedom, from those who are untrustworthy, from those who refuse to respect love. Allow healing to come to those who have been bound, to those who have been weighed down in the prison of a captive relationship.

Lord, I speak freedom, fearlessness, and faith to those who need courage to be free. As well, Lord, I pray that the Jonahs who are thrown overboard will find their place of repentance so they too would be healed and changed to move on to their place in life. Lord, I pray for freedom for everyone, liberty and peace in the Lord. I love You.

Now the Lord is the Spirit, and where the Spirit of the Lord is, there is freedom. (2 Corinthians 3:17 ESV)

Your Way Or His?

The Scriptures clearly direct us to *"lean not on our own understanding" (Proverbs 3:5 NIV).* The Word of God is our steady guide. It will lead us to God, to well-being, to blessings and purpose. Feelings are good, instincts are helpful, and common sense can be useful, but when all is said and done, only *His* Word stands and is true and reliable. Our understanding of things and of life will often lead us astray. Our minds will rationalize good and evil with that ominous, original tendency birthed in the garden, the inclination to be like God.

Human nature will always seek its own way, its own Tower of Babel, its own system of righteousness, of right and wrong. Without God, humanity will always seek man-made idols that cannot speak, that have no power, no life, and no hope. With unwavering faith, we must be willing to walk in the light of His Word, regardless of any directive the world may give us. Trusting *Him* and acknowledging *Him* will always lead to blessings and a guaranteed gracious outcome.

Lord, I pray, may we each choose wisely in the affairs of life, for truly the cost is high, but the reward is precious. Go with God and He will go with you.

Trust in the LORD with all thine heart; and lean not unto thine own understanding. In all thy ways acknowledge him, and he shall direct thy paths. (Proverbs 3:5–6 KJV)

And your ears shall hear a word behind you, saying, "This is the way, walk in it," when you turn to the right or when you turn to the left. (Isaiah 30:21 ESV)

Do It While You Can

"If it is possible, as far as it depends on you, live at peace with everyone" (Romans 12:18 NIV). In making the decision to live according to His Word I am grateful for its clarity. He said what He meant, He meant what He said, and it is forever settled in heaven. I find that in my journey here on the earth there are things that might not ever be settled. Nonetheless, I must take responsibility for myself before God and man in all circumstances and strive to live in peace with as much as is within me.

Pain runs deep when things are left unsettled, unsatisfied, and unstable, yet He remains certain, stable, and true. Therefore I am confident, happy, blessed, and assured when I choose to remain standing with Him, *"For, in Him we live and move and have our being" (Acts 17:28 KJV).* May we each do what we can, while we can, regardless of any contrary wind, for, *"As long as it is day, we must do the works of him who sent me. Night is coming, when no one can work" (John 9:4 NIV).*

Work out your own salvation with fear and trembling, for it is God who is at work in you, both to will and to work for His good pleasure. (Philippians 2:12–13 ESV)

He Keeps Counting

Some days you can think you are down for the count, and then you realize that He keeps counting. We get knocked down sometimes, but glory to God we never get knocked out. We can rise again, we can begin again, and we can do it all over, knowing His mercies toward us fail not. May today be the day that you pull yourself up on the inside, own your truth, get in your lane, and go forward. Go in His strength, for He has granted you grace sufficient to do all things through Christ Jesus.

But we have this treasure in jars of clay, to show that the surpassing power belongs to God and not to us. We are afflicted in every way, but not crushed; perplexed, but not driven to despair; persecuted, but not forsaken; struck down, but not destroyed; always carrying in the body the death of Jesus, so that the life of Jesus may also be manifested in our bodies. (2 Corinthians 4:7–10 ESV)

I will go in the strength of the Lord GOD: I will make mention of thy righteousness, even of thine only. (Psalm 71:16 KJV)

Misunderstood

"But I say unto you, Love your enemies, *bless them that curse you, do good to them that hate you, and pray for them which despitefully use you, and persecute you" (Matthew 5:44 KJV).* As I meditate on the instructions of His Word, I sense deep calling unto deep in the simplicity of the life within Him. He came to help, to heal, and to handle His journey in the earth, with no ulterior motive and no strings attached. He loved selflessly, and He sought to bring change for the better wherever He went. His heart was full of goodness.

It hurts me to think of the good He came to do and how He was mistreated and misunderstood. It's no different today. There are those who come in *His* name, desiring to do good, with a heart like His, extending gracious hands, yet they are mistreated and misunderstood as He was. It's a beautiful, holy matter to see that He never allowed those who hurt Him to change Him. He stayed on target, focused on the matter that really mattered. Let us follow His leading, learn from His example, keep on loving, blessing, doing good, and praying, regardless of the treatment we receive. There is a reward; He is the Reward and the Rewarder. He is the Gift and the Gift giver.

His divine power has granted to us everything pertaining to life and godliness. (2 Peter 1:3 NASB)

"We are not stoning you for any good work," they replied, "but for blasphemy, because you, a mere man, claim to be God." (John 10:33 NIV)

In him was life, and that life was the light of all mankind. (John 1:4 NIV)

Quieted By His Love

There's a sweetness that comes with living life's journey as you hold the Master's hand. Nothing in life can compare to that sweetness, to the loveliness of knowing He is there. As my birthday approaches, I am rendered speechless when I think about where I came from, how I got here, and what He's done for me. I stand in awe at the magnitude of it all, especially knowing He still holds my hand. He took all the shattered pieces, all the seemingly impossible situations, all my heavy burdens, and in exchange, He gave Himself to me.

I'm amazed, I'm puzzled, I'm almost confused, and I wonder, how could He love such a one as me? Who am I that He is mindful of me? The only answer I have comes in the way of tears streaking down my face. There are no words, no intelligent wisdom, just a burst of indescribable, extravagant love. I'm overwhelmed by His love, by His loving kindness, and His longsuffering toward me. At moments like this as I ponder this mystery, I can only hope others will feel the same rush of illogical compassion and undeserved love. It makes no sense other than it makes us feel worthy, accepted, and reassured that we are His and here for a purpose, for such a time as this.

His love is incomprehensible. He is the vine and we are the branches. Apart from Him we can do nothing, and there is nothing I desire to do without *Him*. *His love is impossible to be without.*

My lover is mine, and I am His. (Song of Solomon 2:16 NLT)

The LORD your God is in your midst, a mighty one who will save; he will rejoice over you with gladness; he will quiet you by his love; he will exult over you with loud singing. (Zephaniah 3:17 ESV)

See what great love the Father has lavished on us, that we should be called children of God! And that is what we are! (1 John 3:1 NIV)

No Stopping Him

He loves us more then we can ever imagine. He has engraved us on the palm of His hands and has counted the very number of hairs on our head. He is forever married to the backslider, and none shall pluck us from His hands. I pray we all would know His love in a deeper measure, for truly how deep, how wide, how strong, and how high is His love for you and me. There is none like Him. There is no love like His, and absolutely nothing can separate us from His love. Even when we feel unlovely or undeserving, there is no stopping *Him*, for He still generously pours His love upon us. When love takes you in, everything changes, and your change is found in you allowing Him to take you in.

Father, take us deeper still, to a place in You where there is no distance between Your giving and our receiving, no distance between Your love and our doubt, to that place, Lord, where love supersedes all deprivation, to that place where perfect love abides and casts out all earthly fears. Lord, You are love, the essence of virtue, the life we so silently desire. *Lord*, draw us, draw us, draw us close to You.

And I pray that you, being rooted and established in love, may have power, together with all the Lord's holy people, to grasp how wide and long and high and deep is the love of Christ, and to know this love that surpasses knowledge—that you may be filled to the measure of all the fullness of God.
(Ephesians 3:17–20 NIV)

Love Takes You In

Discovering who He is opens our hearts to true love, and when love takes you in, everything changes. *"My God turns my darkness into light" (Psalm 18:28 NIV).* Anxiety becomes peace, doubt turns into belief, laws turn into grace, weakness becomes strong, the poor become rich, and "No I can't" becomes, "Yes I can" with the power of His love.

Opening our eyes and seeing ourselves for who we are opens our minds, will, and emotions to our absolute need for transformation. Once we see our need, our deficiency and His sufficiency, our eyes have seen the good thing of God, and now we can say, *"I was blind but now I see" (John 9:25 NIV).*

Saints, let us be willing to look inside first before we look at the fault of another. Let's keep our eyes clean, full of light, becoming like Him, embracing one another in the love of Christ. Then we will have loved others, and we will have loved God.

The light of the body is the eye: if therefore thine eye be single, thy whole body shall be full of light. (Matthew 6:22 KJV)

My Inability Is His Greatness

The more I get to know Him, the more I want to be like Him, and the only way to do that is for me to decrease so that He can increase in me. Too many times we can become so full of ourselves that we lose sight of truth and get a false perspective, and before you know it, pride will sneak in; pride will dangerously deceive us and take over our line of sight.

In actuality when we become full of ourselves, we become blind to the infinite possibilities of God. When we rely on our own ability, we become limited and miss out on the infinite potential of grace that overcomes all impossibilities. We must constantly stay humble and never for a moment think we can take the wheel to steer the course of our lives. Let us allow our Maker to choose our course, let Him lead and let us follow. He knows the way that leads to life. It is only when we are small and insufficient in our own eyes that His greatness shines through our lives. It's my heart's desire that He would shine through me and through all of us.

I am the vine; you are the branches. Whoever abides in me and I in him, he it is that bears much fruit, for apart from me you can do nothing. (John 15:15 ESV)

A New Beat

I know my heartbeat, and I know who and what my heart beats for. I remember a time when I felt as though I did not have a heartbeat, but miraculously, something happened. He came into my life. He took my heart of stone and gave me a heart of flesh. Everything changed; my heart started to beat again. I felt alive, I felt the warmth of life again, the excitement of love. I felt that life had a vibration, and I became part of something new, something exciting. I became part of someone who loved me, who knew every part of who I was and was to become. Everything had a new pulse, a new sound, a new beat. My heart had a new song, and that song radiated through my entire being.

With great holy gratitude, I refuse to allow the issues of my heart to interfere or steal the new life imparted to me. I received a second chance, and now, in order to preserve His new life in me, I am determined to make daily decisions that bring truth to my inner parts. I remain completely open for the impartation of His wisdom, which He gives me in His secret place. The heart is deceitful above all things, and who can know it but Him? My heart cry is, *"Let the words of my mouth, and the meditation of my heat, be acceptable in thy sight, O Lord, my strength, and my redeemer" (Psalm 19:14 KJV).* He is the beat of my heart. He is the Potter and I am the clay. He is the Alpha and the Omega. I am because He is.

After those days, saith the LORD, I will put my law in their inward parts, and write it in their hearts; and will be their God, and they shall be my people. (Jeremiah 31:33 KJV)

Therefore if any man be in Christ, he is a new creature: old things are passed away; behold, all things are become new. (2 Corinthians 5:17 KJV)

Time Stops

Scripture clearly tells us, *"In all thy ways acknowledge Him and He shall direct thy paths" (Proverbs 3:6 KJV).* He tells us, *"Be anxious for nothing, but in everything by prayer and supplication with thanksgiving let your requests be made known to God" (Philippians 4:6 NASB).* He instructs us and says, *"Finally, brethren, whatsoever things are true, whatsoever things are honest, whatsoever things are just, whatsoever things are pure, whatsoever things are lovely, whatsoever things are of good report; if there be any virtue, and if there be any praise, think on these things" (Philippians 4:8 KJV).*

As I meditate on His words, I am infused with *His* presence and filled with the essence of who *He* is. It's almost as if time stops and I become one with Him, one with His power, one with His divine love. It seems like I reach His secret place and I don't want to leave, but He lets me go.

After spending this special time with *Him*, in His Word, in His presence, I become more acquainted with Him and with His ways. He keeps me, He settles my heart, and He satisfies my every longing. He covers us with love. He affirms us with His grace and gives us confidence with His awesome power. I stand in awe of You, Lord. We are cared for in deep ways and are perfected in everything that concerns us.

You will make known to me the path of life; In Your presence is fullness of joy; In Your right hand there are pleasures forever. (Psalm 16:11 NASB)

The LORD will fulfill his purpose for me; your steadfast love, O LORD, endures forever. Do not forsake the work of your hands. (Psalm 138:8 ESV)

He Brings Me Back

There are times in life's journey when I feel there is no rhyme or reason for my being, no purpose and no good in the things I'm doing. There are many times when I just want to quit, and then I don't even know what I'm quitting or where I'm going. In these times I must find my way back to Him. It's in times like this we must follow persistently after His Word to hear His voice even the more.

There are many distractions in life ready to pull us away from our source, from our love, need, and peace in God. There is never a time when I do not need Him and never a time when I will not trust His grace to be sufficient. In the deep parts of my being, even when I stray from the center of His presence, I know only He can satisfy my deepest desires, the voids within my soul.

Father, I thank You that I can rest secure knowing that even in my doubt, my fear, and my uncertainty, You are still true to who You are, not relying on who I am or what I do. I am so thankful for Your mercy, that You made me secure to *"know that all things work together for good to them that love God, to them who are the called according to his purpose" (Romans 8:28 KJV).*

Help us, O God, to find Your purpose and to see Your perspective, for truly You are the potter, the Intelligent Designer, the Creator of life.

Lord, show us Your ways, guide us, plant us, and mold us, so that we can become more like You. Our expectation is in You, Lord, and in You alone.

May we all remain pliable in Your hands and find peace to become all You created us to be. We desire to be Your vessels, Your witnesses, Your hands and feet, Your glory in this earth.

You, LORD, are my lamp; the LORD turns my darkness into light. (2 Samuel 22:29 NIV)

Between Faith And Fear

Some nights as I lay listless, unable to sleep, I sense fear trying to grip me, rob me, and shake everything within me. We must choose to cast down every imagination that is not from Him, to think on things that are pure and lovely and cast our cares upon Him, for truly He cares for us. His perfect love casts out all fear, and in the midst of times like this, I am challenged to see His love that is stronger, His Word that is unshakable, and His truth that never changes.

The Enemy is determined to have us question God, even as he did way back in the garden when he asked Eve, "Did God really say?" We must answer the Enemy confidently with God's Word and say, "*Yes,* God did say, *yes,* God will do, and *yes,* God is willing and able."

I pray for all those struggling, halted between faith and fear; Lord, be their strength, be their clarity, be their light, be their way back to truth. I ask You, Lord, to help us fight the good fight of faith, help us to believe Your promises, help us remember You are always with us and that we are never alone. Father, help us in our unbelief. May we be believers, trusting You for all our needs.

Thank You, Lord. Because of You, we are winners, made like You, a people with Your nature, a people who endure to the end. We shall not be moved. We will remain like trees planted by living waters that bring forth fruit in season, fruit that remains … And all because of You.

Jesus answered, "It is written: 'Man shall not live on bread alone, but on every word that comes from the mouth of God.'" (Matthew 4:4 NIV)

And straightway the father of the child cried out, and said with tears, Lord, I believe; help thou mine unbelief. (Mark 9:24 KJV)

Beyond Our Ability

As I look back at some of the impossible situations I and my friends were facing, my heart could only take refuge in knowing Him. Sometimes I get to a place where there are no other options, no other remedies, and no other thoughts that could ease my concerns. When we reach this place that is far beyond our ability to endure, in a way we are fortunate to have no choice but to surrender it all to Him. Often, I could not pray enough, love enough, give enough; all I could do in these times is trust in His love, trust in His mercy and in His ability to make things okay. The truths of His Word that taught me how to live in impossible situations when I felt I could not breathe anymore are the same truths that faithfully keep me day after day. There is none that can pluck us from His hand, none that can separate us from His care. I have learned much, and the greatest lesson I continually learn is the simplicity of simply trusting Him. *"Trust in The Lord with all thine heart; and lean not unto thine own understanding."* (*Proverbs 3:5 KJV*).

Today I encourage each and every one of you to cling to Him, draw close to Him, lean on Him, give Him your burdens, trust Him desperately, stay the course, and let nothing unsettle you or take you from the place of surrender.

He will not disappoint you. He will see you through any circumstance. There is nothing too hard for Him. He will strike the Enemy with overwhelming might to set you free. Fix your mind on His mercy. He is the one who loves you through it all, the faithful one who is ever mindful of you. He has us forever engraved in His hands and forever, untiringly, gives Himself to make intercession for us. He is the only one we run to. He is our God, and we are His people. In God we trust.

We were under great pressure, far beyond our ability to endure, so that we despaired of life itself. Indeed, we felt we had received the sentence of death. But this happened that we might not rely on ourselves but on God, who raises the dead. (2 Corinthians 1:8–9 NIV)

The LORD taketh pleasure in them that fear him, in those that hope in his mercy. (Psalm 147:11 KJV)

Leave It In His Hands

Sometimes plans change, and I have learned not to buck the change because I know the Lord is working for my good behind the scenes. I completely trust my life to Him, in all the small and big moments. If I miss a train, miss a plane, or lose an opportunity, His Word has taught me to trust that He has everything under control. When we trust Him and His sovereignty, all we need to do is our best and leave the rest to His providence.

There are some things in life we just can't change, but if we allow Him to place His hand in our circumstances, a perfect peace will come that transcends all rational thinking, a peace that will go beyond our understanding. Trust will take the fear out of our approach to situations. Trust and you will see life through new eyes—through eyes of hope, through eyes of optimism, through the eyes of a compassionate God who will never leave you or forsake you.

"I know that you can do all things, and that no purpose of yours can be thwarted" (Job 42:2 ESV)

"Even from eternity I am He, And there is none who can deliver out of My hand; I act and who can reverse it?" (Isaiah 43:13 NASB)

He Keeps Me From Falling

Some seasons take me to a place where I feel unglued. God continually teaches me much about making wise choices in the midst of raw emotions. Especially when I am misunderstood, a sense of falling apart strikes a sensitive nerve in my inner being, which then produces these raw and sometimes uncontrolled emotions. In these seasons of feeling unglued, I am kept together by Him and by a divine desire to be a fountain of goodness, kindness, gentleness, faithfulness, and understanding to others who feel misunderstood in their journey. He upholds all things by His Word, and we will not come undone in the midst of feeling unglued. He is always our helper.

"For I am The Lord your God who takes hold of your right hand and says to you, Do not fear; I will help you." (Isaiah 41:13 NIV)

Now unto him that is able to keep you from falling, and to present you faultless before the presence of his glory with exceeding joy. (Jude 1:24 KJV)

Stuff Happens, But So What

At the end of this day while I was thinking, *Yay, it's almost time for this extremely busy day to be over*, there was an unexpected surprise. As I was moving around and bent over, my phone fell out of my pocket and went swimming in the dishwasher. Although I rescued it from the water, hoping it survived, needless to say, it was no longer functional in any capacity.

As I think about this, it reminds me that stuff happens and when it does, you just have to push through. Don't let it grip you, and don't let it get to your heart. When we are living in *Him*, things will come and things will go, but He remains. I am so thankful for all the lessons I learn daily and am determined to stay in His light so I in turn may strengthen the hands and the hearts of those sent to me for comfort and care.

I find it amazing that when I have the right perspective on things, not letting go of His peace, I am able to keep my cool, and life continues to flow uninterrupted by the annoyances and noise in the journey. He is an awesome and wise God who uses all things for our benefit. Being His child makes all things possible, passable, and positively doable. He gives us grace to achieve the impossible, faith to walk on water, and hope to scale the highest mountains.

I am so thankful that in Him I live and move and have my being. It's all because of Him. Thank You, Lord. You are my keeper, my sustainer, my forgiver, my teacher, and the one I love.

Praise be to the God and Father of our Lord Jesus Christ, the Father of compassion and the God of all comfort, who comforts us in all our troubles, so that we can comfort those in any trouble with the comfort we ourselves receive from God. (2 Corinthians 1:3–4 NIV)

You Lead, I Will Follow

When I made a decision to follow Him, there were choices to be made within that decision. As His follower, I recognize never to go before Him, never to go out in front to Him, and never to get too far behind Him. I see many running ahead, and the moment you are in front of Him, you are no longer following Him. I never want to go my own way or desire to do it my way, so I follow Him and stay close, under His covering.

Tonight I pray for all those who feel lost in the journey, that they would find their way back in alignment with Him. I pray for those who are ahead of Him and for those who are so far behind Him that they would find the joy of being in harmony with His direction and not their own. I pray that none would get harmed by kicking against the pricks.

Father, I am thankful You have not left us helpless and without guidance. I say Spirit of the living God, fall fresh on Your people and cause them to arise, to be awakened and come away with their beloved who has called them by name with His sweet invitation, "Come follow Me." May we all find grace to answer, "*Yes*, Lord," to your will, to your way, and to your leading as we follow you all our days in the surrender of your love. Lord, You lead and we will follow.

And Jesus said to them, "Follow Me, and I will make you become fishers of men." Immediately they left their nets and followed Him. (Mark 1:17–18 NAS)

He makes me lie down in green pastures. He leads me beside still waters. (Psalm 23:2 ESV)

Hear Him When He Calls

I hear Him in the beat of my heart, and in every moment I must cherish each beat. As we travel upon this earthly voyage, our opportunities are boundless. Every day is a gift, every heartbeat is a miracle, and in every choice, in every beat, it's vital to hear His voice and know His way. We must walk in His light, in His marvelous light, and not stray from the sacred, ancient path that leads to and offers eternal life. He never changes, and though there be many voices calling for our attention, we must first and foremost recognize the voice of life, the voice of love, the voice that draws us close to Him. Then we must know the imposter's voice that distracts from holy purpose. *"Therefore I have set my face like a flint, and I know that I shall not be put to shame" (Isaiah 50:7 ESV).*

My mind is stayed on Him, with all my hope resting in His promises. He lights my path, embraces my every move, surrounds me as a shield, and catches me when I fall. He lifts me from the miry clay. He is my glory and the lifter of my head. I am His and He is mine, and how true it is, His love shall never fail.

My sheep hear my voice, and I know them, and they follow me. I give them eternal life, and they will never perish, and no one will snatch them out of my hand. (John 10:27–28 ESV)

My Road Map

I love the Word of God. I need the Word of God. Truly it's the road map for my journey. His Word always directs me and never leaves me at a loss for which way to go even when there's a fork in the road. When I follow after His peace, there is never uncertainty. His way is always clear. His Word is always sure. *"The heart of man plans his way, but the Lord establishes his steps" (Proverbs 16:9 ESV).* I am so thankful that God is a personal God to a personal people, and I always want to be up close and personal with Him. He's taught me so much, yet I know there's so much more. As long as I'm alive, my heart will continually long to learn the lessons He gives. Each day there are lessons to be learned, and if I do not learn them, I will never be able to lead others in the way I have not gone. I'm here for such a time as this and choose to live my days in the light of who He is. Tonight my heart sings of His love that leads me on in the journey, for it was His love that changed my life forever.

Through thy precepts I get understanding: therefore I hate every false way. Thy word is a lamp unto my feet, and a light unto my path. (Psalm 119:104–105 KJV)

And we all, with unveiled face, beholding the glory of the Lord, are being transformed into the same image from one degree of glory to another. For this comes from the Lord who is the Spirit. (2 Corinthians 3:18 ESV)

We Have A Comforter

Sometimes we can feel helpless, hopeless, and held back, but we must recognize that it's all lies and we don't have to live by or trust our feelings. The Bible says, *"The just shall live by faith" (Hebrews 10:38 KJV),* and *"Now, faith is the substance of things hoped for and the evidence of things not yet seen" (Hebrews 11:1 KJV).* I encourage you today to know without a doubt that you are not helpless, not hopeless, and not abandoned, for He has sent the Helper, the Comforter from above. You are not hopeless, for hope is our anchor and the anchor holds. We are not held back, for whom the Son sets free is free indeed and nothing shall separate or hold us back from His love.

Hug someone today, and make sure it's a hug from the inside out that changes someone from the outside in and changes both of you by the power of His Spirit. We must stay the course and remind ourselves of His wisdom, not ours.

Then he answered and spake unto me, saying, This is the word of the LORD unto Zerubbabel, saying, Not by might, nor by power, but by my spirit, saith the LORD of hosts. (Zechariah 4:6 KJV)

But the Helper, the Holy Spirit, whom the Father will send in my name, he will teach you all things and bring to your remembrance all that I have said to you. (John 14:26 ESV)

Free To Be Me

I see Him in everything. It's the only way I know how to live! I must get His perspective in all things. If I don't, there's no hope, no reason, no purpose, but with *Him* all things become new. As I went through the baggage check today, I thought of how much baggage I had when I first came to know Him and how I was able to leave it all at the foot of the cross. I am going to make it a practice to check myself daily and to not carry anything He has not called me to carry. There are things I must let go of, and there are other things I must hold tightly.

I pray that each of us would consider our ways and judge our own hearts in the light of His Word and not in the opinions of others. We must discern the times, discern our activities, cast the whole of our care on Him, and take on His yoke, which fits us perfectly. I am so thankful for a life of freedom. I am free, I am free, I am free to see as *He* sees, free to do as He does, free to be the me He created me to be. I am thankful, Lord, that You carry my burdens, that You give discernment to avoid the traps of the Enemy. I am thankful, Lord, for this life of grace You have so freely given that sets me free.

Now the Lord is the Spirit, and where the Spirit of the Lord is, there is freedom. (2 Corinthians 3:17 NIV)

The Son Giver

It wasn't easy leaving our sunny place of rest to return to the cold of winter. I was so grateful for that time of refreshing, renewing, and restoration. *"It is the blessing of the LORD that makes rich, And He adds no sorrow to it" (Proverbs 10:22 NASB)*. I have to be honest, though, in saying I wasn't ready to go, but ready or not, we were going. I am so thankful the Son goes with me everywhere I go.

The Lord has appointed times for us, and even though we may not feel ready for a season or situation, as we trust in God, He always, always gives us grace to not only live through the season but also to profit from all things we go through. When He is the center of our universe, we can profit from all our trials.

I love the sun, but I love the Son more. I love a time of rest, but our true rest is in *Him*. There is never a cloud too thick to cover the glory of *His Son* He gives as we look to *Him*. Let us be thankful and receive grace for a life that enters into *His* rest. His rest heals, loves, and soothes our deepest wounds; His love gives us hope. Let us look to *Him*, the author and the finisher of our faith. He is the Son giver.

The Son is the image of the invisible God, the firstborn over all creation. (Colossians 1:15 NIV)

Keep Your Word; He Does

When you make a vow, keep it and let nothing and no one allow you to get off course. A good name is rather to be remembered than riches, and we will be remembered by the words we have said, kept, and lived by. Better to not make a vow than to make one and then not expect to be held accountable. We are accountable. The Lord made a vow to us that He will never leave us or forsake us, and to this day, He has been faithful to me. He promised to give us new mercies every morning, and every day I wake, He greets me with His love, with new mercies. Actually, God has made many vows and many promises to us, and He keeps them all. Make a vow and keep it. Your truthfulness will be pleasing to God.

For as many as are the promises of God, in Him they are yes; therefore also through Him is our Amen to the glory of God through us. (2 Corinthians 1:20 NASB)

All you need to say is simply 'Yes' or 'No'; anything beyond this comes from the evil one. (Matthew 5:37 NIV)

"Again, you have heard that it was said to the people long ago, 'Do not break your oath, but fulfill to the Lord the vows you have made.'" (Matthew 5:33 NIV)

Cause Me To Hear Your Loving Kindness

Many of us are crying out. In fact, I believe all of us have a special heart cry and desire we are longing for. Sometimes as we wait upon Him, there is great pain in the waiting, but He is always bringing us to deeper levels of understanding and to deeper levels of *Him*. Although His answer may tarry, it is vital that we continue to call out to Him, for He is faithful to answer. It is of no avail to complain, but instead it is good for us to repent of our complaints and take up the cry of faith. He is moved by our dependence on Him and is surely moved by our heartfelt cry of faith. The Bible speaks of those who cried unto *Him*. "*I cried out to The Lord with my voice; with my voice unto The Lord did make my supplication ... I cried unto thee, O Lord: I said, Thou art my refuge and my portion in the land of the living*" (Psalm 142:1, 5 KJV). Cry unto Him, for He promises to hear and comfort you.

This poor man cried, and the LORD heard him, and saved him out of all his troubles. (Psalm 34:6 KJV)

He Hears You,
When You Call

Father, I pray for each one living with a heart cry that pains within them and causes them to feel helpless, hopeless, and hindered from moving forward. Lord, let nothing and no one keep these from hearing You. Lord, let them know they have been heard by the one who is moved into action for those who have put their trust in You. Thank You, Lord, for hearing, for answering, for showing us things we know not, and for delivering us in Your mercy. May Your voice be the loudest in our ears, and may our answer always be, "Yes, Lord, I surrender all."

Cause me to hear thy lovingkindness in the morning; for in thee do I trust: cause me to know the way wherein I should walk; for I lift up my soul unto thee. (Psalm 143:8 KJV)

And this is the confidence that we have in him, that, if we ask any thing according to his will, he heareth us: And if we know that he hear us, whatsoever we ask, we know that we have the petitions that we desired of him.
(1 John 5:14–15 KJV)

The "Nevertheless" Life

I love life regardless of where it takes me. It took an understanding of who He is and the ability to glean His perspective in every issue and in every season to lay hold of the nevertheless life—the life that says, *"Nevertheless I live; yet not I, but Christ liveth in me" (Galatians 2:20 KJV).*

Father, I pray for all those struggling with where they find themselves right now. I pray, Lord, let trust rule and cause peace like a river to flood their every part. May intimacy with You be our heart cry, for it is in that place that we experience the depth of Your love, and it is in that place where we are sound and safe and know all is well, for You are working all things for good. Father, I ask You to raise up people of intimacy with You who will then be instruments of intimacy toward others who long for that in their journey. Life's journey in the earth is fleeting and the brevity of it frail. Help us, Lord, to cherish the importance, the essence of You, and lay aside everything else.

For I have learned to be content whatever the circumstances. (Philippians 4:11 NIV)

For our light affliction, which is but for a moment, worketh for us a far more exceeding and eternal weight of glory. (2 Corinthians 4:17 NIV)

God Doesn't Say Maybe

Things that were so predictable have become unpredictable, and what was normal seems so abnormal now. I am grateful for the place in *Him* where stability is always found and where safety is always present. I am grateful for the grace that allows our yes to be yes and our no to be no, for the place in *Him* where light is light and darkness is darkness. May we all acquaint ourselves with Him, with *His* reality and be at peace knowing His truth is forever sure and certain.

My times are in your hands. (Psalm 31:15 NIV)

What sorrow for those who say that evil is good and good is evil, that dark is light and light is dark, that bitter is sweet and sweet is bitter. What sorrow for those who are wise in their own eyes and think themselves so clever.
(Isaiah 5:20–21 NLT)

For God is not the author of confusion, but of peace.
(1 Corinthians 14:33 KJV)

Let us hold fast the confession of our hope without wavering, for He who promised is faithful. (Hebrews 10:23 NASB)

No Shadow Of Turning With Thee

There are many things I'm not sure of, and all those things have variables. Variables come in a variety of people, places, and things, and it's going to take a refusal of those variable things to live in what is constant. The more I study *His Word*, the greater depth of consistency I understand, and with this understanding as I apply knowledge, the constants in my life become greater than the variables. He is my constant, and my prayer is to consistently become more like Him. God does not waver, so I will not waver. We were created in *His* image and *His* likeness, so why should we settle for anything less? *"As he is, so also are we in this world" (1 John 4:17 ESV).*

I pray that the peace of God, which surpasses all understanding, will enter our hearts and minds to make our steps sure, confident, courageous, and filled with the serenity of God.

Let this mind be in you, which was also in Christ Jesus. (Philippians 2:5 KJV)

Every good thing given and every perfect gift is from above, coming down from the Father of lights, with whom there is no variation or shifting shadow. (James 1:17 NASB)

I Only Have Eyes For You

There is always so much change that comes with each day's journey. I do not understand much of it, and neither do I seek to ask why, for I know what matters most is to keep my eyes on the one who never changes, the one who is the stability of my times. He is the keeper of my heart. He steadies my beat, and I can never thank Him enough. Look to Him at all times. He will guide you, teach you, supply all your needs, watch over you, contend with your enemies, make your paths straight, and make you more like Him. Yes, I can never thank Him enough; Lord, my eyes are on You.

For we are powerless against this great horde that is coming against us. We do not know what to do, but our eyes are on you. (2 Chronicles 20:12 ESV)

He will be the sure foundation for your times, a rich store of salvation and wisdom and knowledge; the fear of the LORD is the key to this treasure. (Isaiah 33:6 NIV)

Footsteps Of Promise

I believe that God uses all of our lives' issues as lessons to instruct us about *Him* and *His* ways. The Enemy will use difficult circumstances to draw us away from God's purposes, but when we follow the Lord's example in the midst of our trials and tribulations, we become more like Him and receive the favor of His promises. The Bible tells us, *"And be not conformed to this world: but be ye transformed by the renewing of your mind, that ye may prove what is that good, and acceptable, and perfect, will of God"* *(Romans 12:2 KJV).*

As we open our minds to God's Word, we will begin to see life through the eyes of faith and the will of God. We will understand that God uses all things for our good, and what the Enemy meant for evil, God will also use for good. Through humility Jesus was led to *His* ultimate victory, and as we trust the Lord with all our being and humble ourselves to His purposes, in due time, we also will be lifted up and ushered into our destiny, to a place of hope and fruitfulness.

Lord, thank You for being faithful. You give us grace each day and forever make intercession for us. Lord, You are our God. You care for us, and there is none like You.

"You intended to harm me, but God intended it all for good. He brought me to this position so I could save the lives of many people." (Genesis 50:20 NLT)

And we know that all things work together for good to them that love God, to them who are the called according to his purpose. (Romans 8:28 KJV)

Lifetime Team Players

The day I accepted Him into my life, I became a lifetime member of His body. It's sad that some who have accepted membership do not really want to participate like members but would rather be lone rangers. We are called to participate with each other in the unity of Christ, as vessels sharing *His* glory. The bible tells us, *"There should be no schism in the body; but that the members should have the same care one for another" (1 Corinthians 12:25 KJV).* We are one in Christ and together as we do our special part, the body of Christ becomes effective in its calling to share God's love, to help those in need, to encourage each other in the faith, and to make disciples of many.

Lord, may we all be team members, helping each other, and let us never forget we are all on the same side, the Lord's side, but more so, He is on our side. Thank You, Lord, for making each of us unique, important, lifetime members with special gifts to enjoy and share with a world in need. We cannot do it alone. You have made us sons and daughters of the living God.

We are many parts of one body, and we all belong to each other. (Romans 12:5 NLT)

Don't just pretend to love others. Really love them. (Romans 12:9 NLT)

Out Of The Old, Into The New

"When I was a child, I spake as a child, I understood as a child, I thought as a child: but when I became a man, I put away childish things" (1 Corinthians 13:11 KJV). As I look at my life, every day I see things that I need to put away, and I know I am not alone. We have been made gloriously new, with new thoughts, new ideas, new hopes, new outcomes, new patterns, and new abilities, so let us grow in the wonderful newness of what we were created to be. Help us, Holy Spirit, to put away anything that hinders us from being marvelously transformed into Your image.

I pray for renewed inspiration and renewed discipline in each life for it takes discipline and inspiration to be a disciple. I pray for an increase of grace to help us arrive at a complete surrender so that every part of our being and all that is within us would cry out, *"Holy, holy, holy unto You. Lord, help us!"* May today be the day of decision where actions are made to put away everything that holds us back from a blessed life in You. We are Yours, Lord. Grace us with a determined Spirit so we may walk in the newness of You in all we think, speak, and do. Peace be unto You.

But we all, with unveiled face, beholding as in a mirror the glory of the Lord, are being transformed into the same image from glory to glory, just as from the Lord, the Spirit.
(2 Corinthians 3:18 NASB)

Lose It And You'll Find It

"And as thy days, so shall thy strength be" (Deuteronomy 33:25 KJV). Father, I pray that in each of our lives we would consider our ways and come to the place where godliness with contentment is great gain. Lord, open the eyes of our hearts, that we may see You in all things. I pray that we would not chase after things that rob us of life, that rob us of strength with no eternal gain. Lord, give us more grace to discern lying vanities that try to lure us into pathways lighted not by You, but instead by artificial light. Lord, You are the true light of the world, and it is only in Your light that we see light. Lord, let us seek Your kingdom and not the kingdoms of this world.

"For the kingdom of God is not a matter of eating and drinking, but of righteousness, peace and joy in the Holy Spirit" (Romans 14:17 NIV).

Lord, give us grace to lose our lives so we may find Yours. Lord, give us grace to overcome evil with good, grace to make You our treasure and not the world. May we all come to a place of contentment in You that adds increase to the time we are here, for truly our days are numbered. Thank You, Lord, for time spent with You and for the assurance of Your faithfulness regardless of the times.

My times are in thy hand. (Psalm 31:15 KJV)

"For whoever wishes to save his life will lose it; but whoever loses his life for My sake will find it." (Matthew 16:25 NASB)

My soul yearns, even faints, for the courts of the LORD; my heart and my flesh cry out for the living God." (Psalm 84:2 NIV)

Been There, Conquered That

In the midst of it all there is God and if we listen we will hear Him. Sometimes it takes shutting off all the lights, all the business, all the stuff and many voices that seek our attention. Often these forces are clamoring to offer an opinion, but often these opinions have no grasp, no understanding or connection to our journey. We have to be very careful what influence we allow in our sphere of influence. I can not live without the Lord's voice in my ear, nor can I ever go without His presence. I am needy and each day my need for Him grows greater as I empty myself of anything, anyone and any area in my life that endeavors to settle for that which is not real, profitable and purposeful. Life is way too short to spend my days longing for that which does not long for me. We must all get to the place of, 'been there, conquered that'. I only desire Him and what He has for me. His grace is sufficient and it is only by His grace that I can get to that place of, Been There, Conquered that.

"My sheep hear my voice, and I know them, and they follow me." (John 10:27 KJV)

'Then Moses said to him, "If your Presence does not go with us, do not send us up from here.' (Exodus 33:15 NIV)

I Shall Not Be Moved

Multitudes, multitudes in the valley of decision; though the Lord is near in our decision making, yet He will not always make our decisions for us. Sometimes the Lord may allow certain events to take place in order to get our attention and to make us aware of a direction, but still the decisions are up to us. He may allow an uplifting event to confirm our direction or even an unpleasant event to make us aware that an adjustment needs to be made. We need to be fixed on His Word, ready to examine our ways to see if we are on or off the course of the Lord. It's very simple: His ways bring life and His blessing adds no sorrow. Our ways will bring strife with much sorrow. He will lead and prompt us, but the choice is ours.

Let's pray: Lord, keep us on Your path, in Your ways, fixed to Your purpose. He will answer that prayer for you with much grace. Today my heart sings, "I shall, I shall, I shall not be moved. I shall be like a tree planted by the water. I shall thrive in the way of the Lord, and I shall not be moved." There is a whole lot of shaking going on, and once again, I declare I shall not be moved because of Him.

I have set the LORD always before me: because he is at my right hand, I shall not be moved. (Psalm 16:8 KJV)

Love And Keep Loving

He has captured my heart and taught me to know what love looks like. I can sing of His love forever, for every day is Valentine's Day. I am captivated by His love that fails not—yes, it never fails. I love Him because He first loved me and purchased my salvation on Calvary's tree. It's difficult for me to even imagine why someone would suffer for me. The joy that was set before Him was so strong, filled with purpose, filled with the love of God, with the energy to please the Father, that it consumed His feelings and enabled Christ to withstand all it took to die for you and me.

When we say we love, we need to think twice about what we mean and what we say. Are we willing to truly love the way Christ loved us? Perhaps the Lord in *His* eternal grace doesn't expect us to die or always suffer for others, but can we have the intention to do good, to give, to go out of our way, to put others before ourselves, to be kind, and to love not just for self but for the wonder of being able to experience joy in the success of others? It is a great privilege to love others with the love of Christ, for when we give *His* love, the love of God will flow through us and replenish our reservoir of hopes and dreams with *His* life. So love and keep loving; you will not be disappointed, for as you give you shall receive.

Three things will last forever—faith, hope, and love—and the greatest of these is love.
(1 Corinthians 13:13 NLT)

Owe nothing to anyone except to love one another; for he who loves his neighbor has fulfilled the law.
(Romans 13:8 NASB)

And hope does not disappoint, because the love of God has been poured out within our hearts through the Holy Spirit who was given to us.
(Romans 5:5 NASB)

He Stabilizes Me

Wintery snow looks so beautiful as it paints the jagged branches of barren trees. My eyes are mesmerized by the whirls of snow creating a blanket of white tapestry on the frozen ground below. This winter sight of light, white, gentle breezes, suddenly blowing patches of snow to and fro, reminds me of how quickly things can change from one extreme to the other.

When I see this quick, radiant change, I meditate on His faithfulness, on His constancy, and on how I can depend upon Him to steady my life. I am grateful that in all my changing seasons, He is the same. He changes not. He is always the same yesterday, today, and forever. Oh how I love Jesus. Oh how I need Jesus. Oh how I need His constant, unchanging, unwavering, predictable, steadfast love that never ceases to uphold me, that never ceases to amaze me.

He is our balance, our firm road, our constant lover who loves us even when we are not able to love *Him*. His love secures us, His love holds us, His love covers us, and His love never fails. Call upon Him to brace you. Call upon Him to embrace you. He will bring you peace, He will uplift you with an undying love. He will love you with a perfect love. He will love you with a love that never gives up, with a love that never fails.

The LORD is good unto them that wait for him, to the soul that seeketh him. It is good that a man should both hope and quietly wait for the salvation of the LORD. (Lamentations 3:25–26 KJV)

This hope is a strong and trustworthy anchor for our souls. It leads us through the curtain into God's inner sanctuary. (Hebrews 6:19 NLT)

For God is love. (1 John 4:8 KJV)

You Can Turn Around

My heart is stirred to pray for those who feel as though they have been going in the wrong direction for so long that it's too late for them to turn around. Father, I pray that your light would shine on every part of their being and wrong thought that seeks to keep them trapped in darkness, in a place that is not virtuous or filled with hope. I pray that Your grace would enable them to open every door, every window, every opportunity in their lives that leads to You and that they open wide their hearts to breathe the fresh air of Your everlasting love and mercy. I pray they would have no worry, no concern, and would not be deceived about time lost as they gain the knowledge that You can redeem their time. Allow them to know of a truth, Lord, that though they may walk east for fifty years, to go west, all they have to do is turn around.

I pray they would surrender everything they are and everything they are not to You, oh God, and that they would trust You to perfect everything that concerns them. Thank You, Lord, that your Word fails not, that You are forever married to those who go astray, and it is never too late for anyone to turn around, to turn back to Your love. Lord, You forgive, You restore, You heal the brokenhearted, You give life to dry bones, You are the repairer of the breech, You set captives free, You take the broken and make them whole. Only You, Lord, make all things new.

And the one sitting on the throne said, "Look, I am making everything new!" And then he said to me, "Write this down, for what I tell you is trustworthy and true." (Revelation 21:5 NLT)

See, I am doing a new thing! Now it springs up; do you not perceive it? I am making a way in the wilderness and streams in the wasteland. (Isaiah 43:19 NIV)

To Be Or Not To Be

Father, I pray for all those who are living with a troubled heart in this hour. You have told us, "*Let not your heart be troubled: ye believe in God, believe also in me*" *(John 14:1 KJV)*. Help us, Lord, to hold back the "*slings and arrows of outrageous fortune.*" Help us, Lord, to hold back the tide of troubles from seeping into the hidden places of our hearts, for this onslaught seeks to steal our prized possessions, our faith, hope, and love. Many are the afflictions of the righteous, but You, oh God, deliver us out of them all. I pray strength for every believer to overcome affliction, for unwavering trust in the Lord's guidance and amazing grace for the troubled heart, so that they may fix their mind on You, Lord, with a steady expectation to be kept in the promise of Your perfect peace.

You will keep in perfect peace all who trust in you, all whose thoughts are fixed on you! (Isaiah 26:3 NLT)

Now may the Lord of peace himself give you peace at all times and in every way. The Lord be with all of you.
(2Thessalonians 3:16 NIV)

See The Warning Signs

Often we do not give proper attention to our beating hearts and the care necessary for the health of them. Scripture instructs us, *"Keep thy heart with all diligence; for out of it are the issues of life" (Proverbs 4:23 KJV).* There are many things in a day that seek to stop my heartbeat that could bring me to a place of fear or hopelessness. Saints, see the warning signs; know that fear is not God's mentality. The Lord gives peace, joy, good gifts, and abundant life, and He desires to give them to you. As long as there is breath, there is hope and truly, *"There is no fear in love, but perfect love casts out fear" (1 John 4:18 ESV).* Stay anchored, keep breathing, and never stop beating to the rhythm of His love.

For God hath not given us the spirit of fear; but of power, and of love, and of a sound mind. (2 Timothy 1:7 KJV)

Thou wilt shew me the path of life: in thy presence is fulness of joy; at thy right hand there are pleasures for evermore. (Psalm 16:11 KJV)

His Word Will Never Return Void

Today is another day in our lives, and regardless what kind of day it is, it is ours and we must choose to live it to the fullest. Life is a gift and also a choice. Scripture teaches that death and life are in the power of our tongues, so we must choose life. I speak words of life, health, and peace over you today, and I pray you will cherish every moment of your days, for we are here for such a time as this. Speak His words.

Speak His intentions. Speak words of encouragement one to another. Speak His ways. Speak His outcomes, His possibilities, and His plans. Speak who He is and who He says you are. Speak goodness, hope, life, love, grace, and peace. Speak words of faith. Speak great expectations. Speak to the mountains in your way. Call those things that are not as though they are. Always speak *His* outcomes and they shall be unto you as you have spoken and believed. Life and death are in the power of your tongue. Therefore allow *Him* to speak life through you. Allow *Him* to direct your thoughts, your words, and your actions. Ask and you shall receive, for it is *His* great desire to do good things through you.

"So shall my word be that goeth forth out of my mouth: it shall not return unto me void, but it shall accomplish that which I please, and it shall prosper in the thing whereto I sent it." (Isaiah 55:11 KJV)

"You will also decree a thing, and it will be established for you; And light will shine on your ways." (Job 22:28 NASB)

Jesus answered, "It is written: 'Man shall not live on bread alone, but on every word that comes from the mouth of God.'" (Matthew 4:4 NIV)

The Brevity of Life,
The Eternity of His Love

I'm thinking about the brevity of life today and thanking Him for giving me a life of purpose. Sometimes I think we take our days for granted and choose to forget that each one of them is numbered. I am determined to make each one count for eternity and to live with destiny on my mind. We all have an expiration date here in this world. It's just not printed on us like it is on a milk carton.

I am thankful that each moment in Him lasts forever. Let us therefore enter in to that place where there is no expiration date—the place where there is peace with God, tthe place of God's presence, the place of God's love. God, help us to live soberly, steadfast, and sure in your call. I am grateful that we may experience eternity, now, in every breath with You.

Whereas ye know not what shall be on the morrow. For what is your life? It is even a vapour, that appeareth for a little time, and then vanisheth away. (James 4:14 KJV)

Now this is eternal life: that they know you, the only true God, and Jesus Christ, whom you have sent. (John 17:3 NIV)

With Or Without You, I'm Going

Sometimes life's journey can take you to a place of wondering who and what to separate yourself from and who and what you need to join yourself to. I believe we are living in an hour where we need to ask ourselves the hard questions and then do whatever is necessary to stay on course with Him. There are so many distractions and things that seek to take us from our place, purpose, and passion. Set your eyes like a flint, know those that labor among you and stay in your lane.

Brethren, I do not regard myself as having laid hold of it yet; but one thing I do: forgetting what lies behind and reaching forward to what lies ahead, I press on toward the goal for the prize of the upward call of God in Christ Jesus.
(Philippians 3:13–14 NASB)

Therefore, since Christ suffered in his body, arm yourselves also with the same attitude, because whoever suffers in the body is done with sin. As a result, they do not live the rest of their earthly lives for evil human desires, but rather for the will of God. (1 Peter 4:1–2 NIV)

All Or Nothing At All

I realize more and more that if I am going to live the nevertheless life, my circle is going to get smaller and I must be okay with that. Not everyone wants to swim upstream against the current, against popular opinion, and not all want to walk the straight and narrow way. It's not easy, and yet when you stay destiny minded, you know that the separated life is the way and the truth of life's journey. My heart's cry is for more of Him, and whoever that separates me from or joins me to is acceptable and embraced, for I need to go deeper, walk closer, and listen. If you listen, He will speak.

Saying, Father, if thou be willing, remove this cup from me: nevertheless not my will, but thine, be done.
(Luke 22:42 KJV)

Deep calls to deep in the roar of your waterfalls; all your waves and breakers have swept over me. (Psalm 42:7 NIV)

Seasoned With Salt

Trust takes time to build. It's built line upon line and precept upon precept. In every day we are given opportunities to build or to break. Every day we get to make choices that have an impact on the heart of another, and that impact will make an imprint that is lasting.

Father, I pray for all those who have been hurt, betrayed, mocked, deceived, and manipulated by another. Lord, I thank You that You understand because You experienced all that and more as You walked to Your destiny, yet Your trust in the Father never wavered. Lord, You maintained your focus and always endured by the love of God for the joy that was set before you. The Lord was *"oppressed, and he was afflicted, yet he opened not his mouth" (Isaiah 53:7 KJV)*. Our words can carry the hope of life or the sting of death, so let us always speak life and hope to others.

Lord, allow the joy of salvation to flood our beings, to overtake our speech, and for healing to flow from our lips. Allow us, Lord, to be instruments of your graciousness, instruments of life. You are our portion, Father, and I pray we will always be your portion, your loving kindness in every opportunity given.

Let your speech always be gracious, seasoned with salt, so that you may know how you ought to answer each person (Colossians 4:6 ESV)

You Have Greatness In You

I live my life with Him on my mind and in my heart, and I am so grateful for the opportunities that arise to be His hand extended toward those who feel like it hurts to breathe or that they cannot breathe again. I remember times when I felt so stressed that I felt like I was holding my breath all the time, and then suddenly there would be someone He would send who would breathe on me and I would hope again. I encourage you today to seek Him and to seek ways to be used by Him. There are so many people who need what you have. Even when you feel like you have nothing, you still have greatness in you to impart. You have Him in you.

If the Spirit of him who raised Jesus from the dead dwells in you, he who raised Christ Jesus from the dead will also give life to your mortal bodies through his Spirit who dwells in you. (Romans 8:11 ESV)

For God wanted them to know that the riches and glory of Christ are for you Gentiles, too. And this is the secret: Christ lives in you. This gives you assurance of sharing his glory. (Colossians 1:27 NLT)

Prepared For The Unexpected

Some seasons are unexpected, uninvited, and unimaginable, yet they come in under the radar. We can think something is over and then there it is again, or we can believe we are over it when suddenly it appears and then tears begin again. I once heard it said, "The times they be a-changing," and yes I have learned to come to terms with change, challenges, and choices that must be dealt with continually.

I remind myself: fear is not of God. Our Lord will not remember our sins. There is no condemnation in Christ, God is a very present help in times of trouble, and we are new creations being transformed daily into His likeness. Things may happen, old patterns may recur, other people who have hurt us in the past may reappear with actions against us, or supposedly healed relationships may become unhealed. Whatever the unexpected event may be, the Lord is forever a constant shield about us, granting us peace and safety, leading us by still waters, and forever making intercession for us. I am so thankful that He is my God and that He will navigate the course in front of us and get us to where He needs us to be. My heart is fixed, and the anchor holds.

Jesus Christ the same yesterday, and to day, and for ever. (Hebrews 13:8 KJV)

He Sees, He Hears

Sometimes life can just leave you speechless, and in those times I am grateful that He interprets my tears. How blessed we are to have a God who sees all, hears all, knows all, and can do all. He knows us most and loves us best, and where He leads I will follow. I pray that each of us will stay anchored because the anchor holds us, and though the storms may rage, He remains our peace that passes all our understanding. He's got us. He won't let us go, and He won't allow us to let *Him* go. Encourage yourself in the Lord, and know that you are not forgotten. Clearly He holds to *His* promise that nothing can separate us from the love of God. He hears our every cry. He speaks to us, calls us by name, searches us, feels our pain, and is acquainted with all our thoughts. He formed us in the womb, and surely we are engraved on the palms of *His* hands.

Behold, I have engraved you on the palms of my hands; your walls are continually before me. (Isaiah 49:16 ESV)

You have kept count of my tossings; put my tears in your bottle. Are they not in your book? (Psalm 56:8 ESV)

It Makes Me Better

As life's journey goes on, I discover that every ending has a beginning and every beginning has an ending while I'm alive in the earth. There will always be change, there will always be opportunities, and there will always be a process we go through in order to get to the other side. Some days it seems as though the process will kill me, and then I realize it's the process that's making me, shaping me, changing me, and molding me as I seek to embrace His will in all things. In all of my losses He has been my gain, and in all of my gain He has still been my gain.

It's vital that we seek His perspective in all things and learn from every life experience so that everything becomes a tool in our hand for His purpose. My pain is kingdom gain, and He will use all of it to bring hope, help, and healing to others in their life process. He will make all things beautiful in His time, and we can rejoice that He uses us to do it. I'm amazed that although there is a beginning and an end in this lifetime, our lives with Him are forever. We are a fortunate, blessed, favored, forever people in His care. I love you.

For he chose us in advance, and he makes everything work out according to his plan. (Ephesians 1:11 NLT)

Invest Wisely

I believe life is about making investments, and without an investment, there has to be an understanding that there will be no return. When I was a kid, I would invest my time walking around with a shopping cart collecting bottles to return for money. It was worth it to me, so I put the time in. My life now is about making deposits and investments in people, and the return of seeing them saved, hopeful, hugged, accepted, loved, and grateful is priceless. I have one life to live just like you, and I encourage you to live it selflessly and make deposits that will last for eternity.

One person gives freely, yet gains even more; another withholds unduly, but comes to poverty. A generous person will prosper; whoever refreshes others will be refreshed. (Proverbs 11:24–25 NIV)

Imagine There's No Heaven

Can you even for a moment imagine life without Him?
There would be no hope for a future, no promise for the
here and now or for the ever after, no light, no laughter,
no joy, no air to breathe, no tears to cry, no sounds to
hear, no love to share, nowhere to go, no road to travel.
There would just be nothing without Him, but He gives
us everything. He simply says, *"Ask, and it will be given to
you" (Matthew 7:7 ESV)* because He loves you.

I love Him, and I look to Him for everything I have and
want to be. Knowing Him is why I am able to endure
hard times because I am certain of His faithfulness,
His motives, and His plan. He has never left me empty-
handed, and He never will. He always cares for us and
always provides a way of escape. He is our beginning, He
is our end, and I delight in trusting Him through it all.
His purpose is my life's desire. *No*, I cannot imagine life
without Him. Look to Him; He will lighten your burden.
He will see you through. He will make the crooked places
straight, the dark places bright. Trust in Him. He will do
it because He loves you.

*Those who know your name trust in you, for you, LORD,
have never forsaken those who seek you. (Psalm 9:10 NIV)*

This Little Light Of Mine

In my weakness He is strong, and knowing He is with me makes all the difference. As I look around my neighborhood, which is in complete darkness from a blackout, my heart rejoices that He is the light that never goes out. He illuminates my darkness, not only for me but for those around me, that when they see me, they will see Him. The Lord our God in the midst of us is mighty, and we cannot allow that to slip away from us during trying times. If we all do our part as His body and supply to each other what we can, then there will be no lack.

His gift of prayer makes transforming power available for ourselves and to those we are praying for. Giving what we have strengthens the weak, gives hope to the hopeless, and gives purpose to those who have no vision. Our words will heal and will make the unloved feel loved. I remember the day I was serving at a shelter; the rush of joy I received was unspeakable. The world did not give it to me, and the world cannot take it away. "This little light of mine, I'm gonna let it shine."

In the same way, let your light shine before others, that they may see your good deeds and glorify your Father in heaven. (Matthew 5:16 NIV)

A Home-Cooked Meal

There is nothing that compares to a word in season
fresh from the heart of God. There is such a big difference
between a message and a word from Him. I compare them
to fast food against a home-cooked meal. I am grateful I
was taught to burn the midnight oil, to seek Him with my
whole heart, and to never let go of or not depend on His
Spirit to deliver a life-changing word from His throne of
grace. When you drink His waters, you will never thirst,
and when you eat His Word, you will never go hungry. He
is constantly speaking and always leading us into truth. I
will never stop listening and never stop following.

*Then the LORD called Samuel. Samuel answered, "Here I
am." (1 Samuel 3:4 NIV)*

*In the beginning was the Word, and the Word was with God,
and the Word was God. (John 1:1 KJV)*

He Never Disappoints

In the day, and in the night season, my soul yearns for Him as my spirit hungers for Him. He fills all my needs and satisfies my deepest desires. He will not leave you hungry, He will not leave you thirsty, and He will not ignore your heartfelt pleas. He hears and answers when we ask. He knows when you seek Him and makes Himself found, and He opens the door when you knock. The Lord is truly our Jehovah Jireh; He will provide a ram in the bush and will never disappoint you when your trust is in Him. Fear may come, worry, anxiety, or unrest may try to surround you, but He is our sure shelter, in and from the storm.

He teaches us to meditate on His Word, to encourage ourselves in His love, for He changes not yet has the ultimate power to change all things. In the wee hours of the morning and the deep hours of the night, let us know that: *"I lie down and sleep; I wake again, because the LORD sustains me" (Psalm 3:5 NIV).* Let us be comforted, assured, and sustained by the one who is in us, by the only one who is faithful until the end. He will always be there for you.

The righteous cry, and the LORD heareth, and delivereth them out of all their troubles. (Psalm 34:17 KJV)

Everlasting Arms

"The spirit of a man will sustain his infirmity; but a wounded spirit who can bear?" (Proverbs 18:14 KJV).
I am so thankful that He sustains me, keeps me, and tells me I am His own. It is vital that we grasp the understanding of maintaining a strong spirit in the journey regardless of where it takes us, for truly it is where our sustenance comes from. The question, "A wounded spirit who can bear?" I believe is answered by the spirit of the person who knows Him, runs to Him, and who always casts his cares on Him. His love is made perfect in our weakness, and when we are weak, He makes us strong. Keep leaning on Him, knowing He's got you and will never let you go. As the hymn writer exclaimed, "Leaning, leaning, safe and secure from all alarms; Leaning, leaning, leaning on the everlasting arms."

The eternal God is your refuge, and underneath are the everlasting arms. (Deuteronomy 33:27 NIV)

Be merciful to me, O God, be merciful to me, for in you my soul takes refuge; in the shadow of your wings I will take refuge, till the storms of destruction pass by.
(Psalm 57:1 ESV)

This Is The Day

Every day in life's journey is unique to itself. I find it vital not to look at my days as the same old, same old thing but instead with great expectation. Every day is a precious gift, filled with promise, hope, life, His presence, grace, and especially with the mercies of God. There is nothing impossible with God in each day, and there is nothing He will withhold from those He loves. Every day is filled with awe, with His glory, with new opportunities, with new things to see, new things to hear, new lessons to learn, and new seeds to sow. When we remain open to the new occurrences of each day we will find them because He will make sure that they find us.

In some days you just have to look yourself in the mirror and ask yourself with great expectation of a response the questions David asked in *Psalm 42:11 (KJV)*, *"Why art thou downcast, O my soul? and why art thou disquieted with me? hope thou in God: for I shall yet praise him, who is the health of my countenance, and my God."* We must live while we can, work while we are able and find Him in all times. There is hope and surely a "yet praise" on the inside of us yearning to be let out despite the battle. Praise Him! He desires to be revealed in your expression, in your thankful reaction to the life He daily provides.

When you do Praise Him for what He gives, others will see Him and also give thanks for all the goodness He creates. They too will call out with an ecstatic praise, saying, *"This is the day that the Lord has made. Let us rejoice and be glad in it" (Psalm 118:24 ESV).* It doesn't get much better.

For the LORD God is a sun and shield: the LORD will give grace and glory: no good thing will he withhold from them that walk uprightly. (Psalm 84:11 KJV)

Sing to the LORD, bless his name; tell of his salvation from day to day. (Psalm 96:2 ESV)

Never Say Never

Each day as the sun rises and a new day begins, I must be willing to arise with it and embrace the day. There is hope in every moment of every day. There is a divine exchange in every breath, a wonder in every experience, a purpose in every event, and the life of God in all we do. Be aware of Him, listen for His voice, see His light in our waking, feel His comfort all around you, and know His heartbeat in your soul. He is with you and will never leave you.

I remember when I lived in a state of numbness and felt like I was a dead woman walking. I am so thankful that the same spirit that raised Christ from the dead lives in me and quickens my mortal body. Life's journey is a learning experience, and we must learn to keep living, keep believing, keep trusting, and never stop hoping.

I stand with you today to never speak "never" over your life again because many times in doing so your "never" robs you of your future. Speak virtuous, life-giving power from His Word, speak His sure and certain promises over your life, receive the miracle energy of God, and then break through into a life of destiny, a life of hope, of hope fulfilled.

Furthermore, because we are united with Christ, we have received an inheritance from God, for he chose us in advance, and he makes everything work out according to his plan. (Ephesians 1:11 NLT)

Do It
(The Time Is Now)

When you make a vow, keep it, and when you make a decision to do something, it's important to follow through. Too many times we let precious thoughts and deeds to be done or seeds to be planted pass us by, and we miss the timing of our visitation to be a blessing and to get the job done. There is a special timing to everything in life, and there is also a special grace given in the appointed time. I encourage you today to not let these ordained moments of opportunity pass you by, for we know not the desperation of others who will thrive with your seed or the weak who will be revived by what you have in your hand, which was placed there by Him. Stop to listen, hear His voice, and don't doubt that which you know to do or withhold good while it is within you to do it.

There is an appointed time for everything. And there is a time for every event under heaven. (Ecclesiastes 3:1 NASB)

For we are God's handiwork, created in Christ Jesus to do good works, which God prepared in advance for us to do. (Ephesians 2:10 NIV)

Are You Kicking Against The Pricks?

Change comes to us all, and it's a constant in our journey. The decision we get to make in the change is whether we will change for the better or not and whether we will do it our way or His way. If we're going to change for the better, seeing the bigger picture, then we must be determined to live with destiny in our hearts. I also believe change is personal and not dependent on what someone else does or does not do. When Christ said to the apostle Paul, *"It is hard for thee to kick against the pricks" (Acts 26:14 KJV),* Christ was saying, "Why are you fighting against My will?" Saints, in every day we have a chance to surrender for a better, higher purpose. Let's reflect and decide not to inflict further pain on ourselves, but instead let's choose His will and move toward our blessed destiny in Christ Jesus.

Saul, Saul, why are you persecuting me? It is useless for you to fight against my will. (Acts 26:14 NLT)

But seek ye first the kingdom of God, and his righteousness; and all these things shall be added unto you.
(Matthew 6:33 KJV)

They're Waiting for You

We meet lots of people in our journey, from different places, all kinds of spaces, and most of us are running different races. I believe kindness, understanding, and a hearing ear are most important features as we reach out to a world He died for, to a world He loves. As I listen, I hear Him, I hear the need, and I ask for grace to make Him known in whatever I do, wherever I go, for He seeks to meet the need. He says, *"Ask, and it shall be given you; seek, and ye shall find; knock, and it shall be opened unto you" (Matthew 7:7 KJV).* We are not alone as we go, but we are encouraged to go on. *"Wherefore seeing we also are compassed about with so great a cloud of witnesses, let us lay aside every weight, and the sin which doth so easily beset us, and let us run with patience the race that is set before us" (Hebrews 12:1 KJV).* I don't know what's set before you, but I do know we all have something before us, and I pray that regardless, we will be settled in His will and surrendered to His purpose, knowing He will answer your prayer, open a door, bring you peace, give you hope, and yes, He will answer your prayer while making you the answer for another.

For the creation waits in eager expectation for the children of God to be revealed. (Romans 8:19 NIV)

I Did It My Way

I have seen so many lives thrown into confusion and destroyed by making a decision that takes things into their own hands. Jonah didn't agree with God's way of thinking and ended up in the belly of a whale with seaweed wrapped around his neck. Adam and Eve wanted to be like God. They fell for that deadly temptation and messed things up in a big way, and Uzzah was slain when he tried, even with good intentions, to keep the ark from falling. I wonder how we get to the place of, *I'll do it my way* or *I know what's best*. A fool says there is no God, and it's foolish to think you know what's best. *"There is a way which seems right to a man, But its end is the way of death"* *(Proverbs 14:12 NASB).*

We see through a glass darkly and we only know in part, so we are bound to get lost without the other part—God's part. We must recognize that the part we know is only a piece and our peace and progress are only found by humbly accepting His counsel and staying under the umbrella of His divine love. I desire to stay surrendered; I'm done with doing things my way. It doesn't work. Give your life to Him and He will direct your paths.

I am the LORD your God, who teaches you to profit, who leads you in the way you should go. (Isaiah 48:17 ESV)

I Look To You

Boundaries are something we all need at every age, and having them sustains well-being for everyone. I see too many living without boundaries, with blurred lines, and I wonder how and why. I need strong boundaries, clear lines, and constants I can count on. It really is the simple way, and that's the way for me. When it gets complicated, you can count me out. I need to hear His voice to follow confidently along His path. I need to feel His hand guiding me along the way. I will even adore a strong poke that keeps me in the reality of His ways and not mine. I will stay close to Him and not lag far behind, and neither will I move ahead beyond His time. "I look to You, I look to You." I love You, Lord. Be my guiding light. "I look to You."

Whether you turn to the right or to the left, your ears will hear a voice behind you, saying, "This is the way; walk in it." (Isaiah 30:21 NIV)

Neither know we what to do: but our eyes are upon thee. (2 Chronicles 20:12 KJV)

I look to you for help, O Sovereign Lord. (Psalm 141:8 NLT)

Unchangeable

I must be able to find Him in the midst of chaos and know that He is faithful. It can often be easy to lose sight of the fact that He is the same God that we find in the same place regardless of the season. The Lord will never forsake you. My instinct in God tells me that in difficult situations my only choice is to become mentally prepared by allowing His peace to surpass all my understanding. Regardless of the circumstance, it's always the certainty found in Him that will guard our hearts and minds against all fear.

He is unchangeable, constant, and faithful in every season, in every way, in every day, and a healer and a lover; that's just His nature. How he was yesterday, He will be today, full of life, overflowing with blessings, and a keeper of His promises. I rely on Him because of His constancy, and every time I go to Him, I know what to expect: His goodness, His mercy, His faithfulness, His love, and the magnitude of His grace that is always more than sufficient. May we each rest assured in His promises, anchored in His love, and never lose His song in our heart. He is our beloved, and we are His.

You are my hiding place; You preserve me from trouble; You surround me with songs of deliverance. (Psalm 32:7 NASB)

Behind The Scenes

Life is beautiful and full of wonder, so I wonder why at times we lose sight of Him working behind the scenes. I know how hard it can get and know how hope can seem to drift away, yet we must remember that He is the anchor that holds and never lets go. When we don't see visible proof, we can take advantage of the glorious opportunity to praise Him for what He's doing that we do not see. We know that the just shall live by faith and not by sight, so in times where there may seem to be no hope or no intervention by our God, we should rejoice in the opportunity to love Him even when we do not see Him. It's easy to be joyful or hopeful when things are going great, but miracles happen when we wait on the Lord, Praise Him and eventually see that. *"Faith is the substance of things hoped for, the evidence of things not seen" (Hebrews 11:1 KJV).* Saints, stay connected to the hope of God and see the promises of God arise in your circumstances. *God never disappoints.* Hallelujah! My help comes from Him.

Then Elisha prayed and said, "O LORD, please open his eyes that he may see." So the LORD opened the eyes of the young man, and he saw, and behold, the mountain was full of horses and chariots of fire all around Elisha. (2 Kings 6:17 ESV)

And this hope will not lead to disappointment. For we know how dearly God loves us, because he has given us the Holy Spirit to fill our hearts with his love. (Romans 5:5 NLT)

While we look not at the things which are seen, but at the things which are not seen: for the things which are seen are temporal; but the things which are not seen are eternal. (2 Corinthians 4:18 KJV)

No Doubt We Are His

In the stillness of the night I see Him in the beauty of His creation, and in His whisper He reminds me that I also am the beauty of His creation. To be part of Him, like Him, created in His infinite image gives me perspective for life. His potential in us is boundless, offering possibilities of grace and hope everywhere we shine His light. Before I was even formed in the womb, He conceived me. He knew me, hand-fashioned me, and placed His heartbeat and fingerprint inside and upon me. Now I know Him who created me, changed me, and called me to be His own. There is no greater love than His, no greater light than Him, and no other way than His will be done. I know the way I shall go because He directs me with His love. He leads me besides still waters and draws me closer to Him with every step I take. We have been made His and joyfully His.

For since the creation of the world God's invisible qualities—his eternal power and divine nature—have been clearly seen, being understood from what has been made, so that people are without excuse. (Romans 1:20 NIV)

Kindness

There are many people I meet in my journey, and kindness is something I find rare. Yesterday I was fortunate to sit with someone who simply sought to be kind, and her kindness made me weep and wonder why there isn't more kindness in this world. I pray that long after I'm gone I will be remembered for showing kindness to others. Kindness is beautiful. Jesus was the epitome of kindness, giving His life so that we might have life. Kindness heals, it brings hope, will melt a bitter heart, dry our tears, and bring energy to a lifeless soul. Kindness brings light to our darkness, new vision to dry places, and vigor to stagnant dreams. Kindness will make life worth living again. It will open our eyes to see new vistas. It will make us sing, bring us joy, and make us see ourselves made in the image of our God. Be kind and you shall reap what you sow—a life of kindness, a life of hope.

Give thanks to the LORD, for He is good, For His lovingkindness is everlasting. (Psalm 136:1 NASB)

But when the kindness and love of God our Savior appeared, he saved us, not because of righteous things we had done, but because of his mercy. (Titus 3:4–5 NIV)

Mountain Mover

When discontentment tries to settle in and make its home in you, don't give in. God is with you. Rise up and remember that, *"Godliness with contentment is great gain, for we brought nothing into the world, and we cannot take anything out of the world"* (1 Timothy 6:6 ESV). Disappointments will come to us and seek to take us from our appointment with Him. Often they will cause us to miss the time of our visitation by focusing on disappointment rather than His appointed time of destiny. Do not allow disappointments to be a repetitive cycle but rather break the cycle with divine confidence by decreeing God's promises over your life: *"If God be for us, who can be against us?" (Romans 8:31 KJV). "Those who sow with tears will reap with songs of joy" (Psalm 126:5 NIV).* Disappointments may come, but God will never disappoint us. He is always acting in our best interest and will always bring us something better and to a better place in *Him*. He loves you and will move mountains in your way.

"I will go before you and will level the mountains; I will break down gates of bronze and cut through bars of iron."
(Isaiah 45:2 NIV)

A Divine Reversal

Didn't the Lord reverse some commonly held concepts of *success* and *greatness* when He said, *"The greatest among you will be your servant" (Matthew 23:11 NIV)?* Jesus brought about a new order, a new set of principles, a new covenant that for some may be hard to follow but easy for those who accept *Him*. It makes me sad to see so many looking for servants when the greatest joy in life comes from being the one who serves. Jesus proclaimed, *"It is more blessed to give than to receive" (Acts 20:35 KJV).* Being favored by serving is echoed in Jesus's mind-set that, *"Whoever exalts himself will be humbled, and whoever humbles himself will be exalted" (Matthew 23:12 ESV).*

In every day there's a mouth to feed, a heart to touch, a need to supply, a person to love. Be blessed to be a blessing, and joyfully do whatever your hand and heart find to do. When you leave someone's presence, make sure they know you were there. Be present when you are present, and serve with grace and gladness. Follow in His footsteps, and wash the feet of those within your reach.

And he sat down and called the twelve. And he said to them, "If anyone would be first, he must be last of all and servant of all." (Mark 9:35 ESV)

So Also Are We

Awakened by a sound, I am ever so aware of His Presence. As I check on my daughter who is fast asleep, and as I pronounce blessings upon her, I hear His whisper. His sound is so gentle, so firm, so real, so kind, so present, all in a whisper I hear His essence. Not in the strong wind, not in an earthquake, not in the fire, but in the sweet, sweet sound of His gently blowing wind. He is a God who always cares, and regardless the times He has made my feet like hind's feet, and He says, "Go, for I am with you." My heart has He changed from a heart of stone to a heart of flesh, and my eyes He has opened that I might see His glory. Oh what beauty to behold. It leaves me speechless, breathless, yet it fills me with unending hope.

I love Him because He first loved me, and I will forever sing of His love, tell of His goodness, and seek to be an expression of Him in this earth. He lives in me. He is the light of my world, the light of the world. *"In him was life, and that life was the light of all mankind" (John 1:4 NIV).* So I bring with me His life, His love, His presence, His mercy, and His grace. I bring Him with me in all that He is, for He makes us like Himself: radiant, loving, glorious, and eternal, overflowing with abundant life, the one who never stops giving.

"And the glory of the LORD will be revealed, and all people will see it together. For the mouth of the LORD has spoken." (Isaiah 40:5 NIV)

We know how much God loves us, and we have put our trust in his love. God is love, and all who live in love live in God, and God lives in them. (1 John 4:16 NLT)

By this is love perfected with us, so that we may have confidence for the day of judgment, because as he is so also are we in this world. (1 John 4:17 ESV)

My Getaway

It's hard to think when your head is clogged and hard to hear when your ears hurt from all the pressure and clanging. On days like this, I am so grateful for being able to think and hear from the inside out. It's during these times of pause that I hear His whispers ever so near and clear. It's like finding a secret place of rest where no one can find you, where no one can bother you, where nothing can harm you. I am learning to travel inward, into that perfect place of peace, where I find Him and Him alone. When I get there, I'm amazed to find more calm, more power, and more love than I could ever have imagined. All you have to do is rest in Him, the one whose love will never fail. Peace be with you. He is our God.

He that dwelleth in the secret place of the most High shall abide under the shadow of the Almighty. (Psalm 91:1 KJV)

"Behold, the kingdom of heaven is within you."
(Luke 17:21 KJV)

The LORD hath appeared of old unto me, saying,
Yea, I have loved thee with an everlasting love:
therefore with lovingkindness have I drawn thee.
(Jeremiah 31:3 KJV)

Why My Heart Beats

On August 26, 1977, I walked down the aisle at Nutley Assembly of God and knelt at the altar to receive Him as my personal Lord and Savior. I had read my Bible for two years, and I had sat in church services for four months getting to know Him before that night. It was not a quick decision or an uninformed one as I needed to know within me if I could trust Him after having been failed so many times and suffering the betrayal of so many.

On that day, as I walked the seemingly long aisle all by myself, my insides were leaping, exhilarated with new hope, with a new vitality I have not known before those moments. Something in me came alive, like a distant, almost lost desire suddenly became fulfilled. Life changed, things looked different, sounds were apparent, light was flickering, and I was lifted into another realm, into the realm of His glory. I just knew that He was all I had ever longed for, all I ever needed, and I knew with all that was in me that He would never fail me or fall short on His promises. I will never forget one of the sisters meeting me at the altar, praying with me and for me. As I wept in her arms, my tears diffused the piercing light of His love that was flowing all over and around me.

It was an awakening, a breaking, a shattering of old delusions, and an entrance into a new life, a living hope, a glimpse of eternity in the moment. Today I rejoice in the gift of salvation and the adventure of living life with Him from the inside out.

'I say to the LORD, "You are my Lord; apart from you I have no good thing." (Psalm 16:2 NIV)

"For God so loved the world, that he gave his only begotten Son, that whosoever believeth in him should not perish, but have everlasting life." (John 3:16 KJV)

For in him we live, and move, and have our being. (Acts 17:28 KJV)

Acknowledgments

In every heart there is much that is gathered along this journey called life.

I am eternally grateful to each person who has watered me along the way and truly there are too many to mention. God has used all of you and although you are nameless here He knows who you are. To all those who have responded to my messages and cheered me on with the grace and enthusiasm I needed to make these words come alive in print, I pray that He grants you every desire of your heart and that you continue to live surrendered to Him in all that you think and do. May your hearts always beat for the one who gave you a heartbeat.

Life's journey is amazing as it brings many people along our path who give of themselves in Christ like ways to accomplish the dreams of another. I am especially indebted to Krystal Boodram and Julio Vitolo, and I could never thank them enough for the countless hours they spent on this project.

Krystal, you have amazed me from a young age, and even now I am still astounded at how God connected our lives and helped us to help each other. We are truly blessed and highly favored to be in the kingdom for such a time as this. Thank you from my heart for always being there for whatever and whenever I needed you. You are a jewel and you shine from the inside out.

Julio, your devotion to Him and your willingness to help others fulfill their calling speaks of your relationship with Him. You have a true gift of encouragement and you are a man after God's own heart. Thank you for the many sacrifices you have made of your time, talent and treasure within. I rejoice that your best days are in front of you and I know your latter will be greater.

I am ultimately grateful to our Lord for giving me the desire, grace, timely words, and energy to manifest these uplifting thoughts for the sake of myself and others.

When I started writing these HeartBeats, I never realized how much they would bless me and bless others. I am amazed, I am humbled, I am grateful and I pray that these messages will continue to bring you hope, joy and the grace you need as you continue to travel on your journey with the Lord. There are many things that seek to capture and stop our hearts but in the end God gets the last word, the promise of hope and the promise of a future. Keep Beating! I love you, Gale .

"For I know the plans I have for you", declares the Lord, "plans to prosper you and not to harm you, plans to give you hope and a future." (Jeremiah 29:11 NIV)

About The Artist

The cover illustration was painted by Noelle S. Gibbons. It was inspired by a photo image spontaneously captured by the author Gale Alvarez.

Noelle S. Gibbons has been drawing ever since she could pick up a pencil ! At an early age Noelle knew she wanted to use her God given gift for His glory. Noelle is a commission artist, a private teacher and has illustrated *'The Lowdown On The High Bridge'* children's book. At the Gordon School of Art in Wisconsin and at the Mary Muller Studio, Noelle was fortunate to cultivate her gift by learning to paint and teach in the technique of the masters. She is blessed to live in Iowa with her husband and young son.

Noelle's Website: Artbynoelle.com

About the Creative Associate
Krystal Boodram

Krystal Boodram's passions have led her in a number of directions with the same common thread centered in a love for her creator. She graduated from Fordham University with a Bachelor of Science Degree in Biology and an English minor. After working in a lab researching E. coli she realized that she was more zealous about the pursuit of people than the pursuit of information. She joined the organization Teach For America and became a teacher in hopes of becoming part of the systemic change necessary to end the cycle of emotional and economic poverty in America.

Krystal is also a contributing music writer for New York Minute Magazine because she recognizes that music is powerful and can instantly transcend any speech or lesson to hit a harmonizing chord with the listener's soul.

Krystal also does extensive volunteer work with her church and believes that her passions come to life by being planted in the House of God and submitted to His will. No matter what role she plays, her goal is that every person she encounters realizes his or her great value stemming from their great Creator.

About the Creative Associate
Julio Vitolo

Julio Vitolo grew up in the Bronx, NY, not too far from the Yankee Stadium. He graduated from the City College of New York with a degree in Music and Early Childhood Education. As a "corridor teacher" in an innovative Manhattan school setting he acquired a keen instinct to recognize and develop the unique gifting within each child.

Subsequently, he applied his creative, educational instincts to business and successfully helped people image, develop and market their special interests.

Julio gives credit to his early educational roots: *Inspiring & nurturing children, has taught me how to identify, "brand" and develop something tangible from a seed of an idea to completion.*

As an inspired Saxophonist, Julio shares his spiritual inclinations through his gift of music. In all his endeavors he is passionate about touching others with the Love of God and is instinctively driven to help others reach their full, God given dreams and potential.

Julio's Facebook Page is: Julio Vee

About the Author, Gale Alvarez

Gale Alvarez is the cofounder of the Love of Jesus Family Church in Orange, New Jersey. The ministry formally began over twenty-seven years ago as Gale and her husband, Pastor Jason Alvarez, traveled extensively with Evangelists R. W. Shamback, Nicky Cruz, and other vibrant ministries.

With her eye on restoration, Gale also founded the Women of Purpose ministry and the T.O.P project, Teens of Purpose ministries at the Love of Jesus Family Church.

Gale Alvarez is a dedicated wife, mother and a gifted minister of God's Word. Gale's sensitivity and insightful understanding of human frailty have supernaturally equipped her to transcend diverse cultures with an uncanny ability to restore identity, wholeness, and wellness to the lives of the broken. Gale Alvarez is eternally dedicated to meeting the spiritual, material, and emotional needs of all people.

Gale Alvarez has been known to be blazing with the Holy Spirit. Her words are filled with the passion, healing balm, and the unconditional love of Jesus.

When Gale speaks, she speaks into the God-given DNA, destiny, and potential of an individual. The body of Christ is blessed to have her gift that nurtures the manifestation of Jesus Christ on this earth.

Her gifting gives life to God's purpose of "being conformed to His image," and her supernatural gift of encouragement restores broken dreams and infuses life into dead bones.

She is truly a needed, Jesus life-giver to the body of Christ. Surely, like Christ, she has learned obedience from what she suffered. One day a hurting saint of God wrote a letter about Pastor Gale's future visit, writing:

"Jesus is coming to see me."

Gale welcomes your responses and would love to hear from you. You can email Gale at:

Galewop@aol.com GalesHeartBeats@aol.com

Gale's Face Book Page is: Heart Beats

Gale is also available for speaking engagements and can be contacted at: 973 676 4200

The Story Behind The Cover

I've always loved sitting at the ocean's edge, looking out into the distance, wondering how the water, so deep and vast, would know just how far to go before it would settle down and gently come to a stop. It amazed me.

I remember the day I took this photo. It's vivid in my mind. I was sitting in my beach chair when all of a sudden I was inspired to get up to write something in the sand. As I walked closer to the water I bent over and started to draw a heart in the sand. When I finished drawing I took a simple photo of the heart. To my surprise it was not until I looked at the photo that I realized what I had captured in that moment. The rushing water, in one swift moment, entered the frame of the photo. The water was rushing toward me but I didn't know that was happening. My footprint was so close to the hand drawn heart that it too, along with the heart, was very close to being washed away by the rushing water.

As I looked at the photo I began to weep realizing that life's journey is just that fleeting. Every single beat of our heart is precious, priceless and we must not allow ourselves to ever take a beat for granted. It's our beating heart that gives us life and just as my footprint made an impression in the sand so I want my life and your life to leave others with an image of Him.

I encourage you to live your life on purpose and not to allow your moments, like the rushing water, to enter your life leaving your days with nothing left behind.

I didn't realize at the time that this image would inspire the cover for my book, **HeartBeats**.

Personal HeartBeats

_____
_____
_____
_____
_____
_____
_____
_____
_____
_____
_____
_____
_____
_____
_____
_____
_____
_____
_____
_____
_____
_____
_____
_____
_____
_____
_____
_____
_____
_____

Personal HeartBeats

_____

_____

_____

_____

_____

_____

_____

_____

_____

_____

_____

_____

_____

_____

_____

_____

_____

_____

_____

_____

_____

_____

_____

_____

_____

_____

_____

_____

Personal HeartBeats

_____

_____

_____

_____

_____

_____

_____

_____

_____

_____

_____

_____

_____

_____

_____

_____

_____

_____

_____

_____

_____

_____

_____

_____

_____

_____

_____

_____

_____

_____

Personal HeartBeats

_____

_____

_____

_____

_____

_____

_____

_____

_____

_____

_____

_____

_____

_____

_____

_____

_____

_____

_____

_____

_____

_____

_____

_____

_____

_____

_____

Personal HeartBeats

_____

_____

_____

_____

_____

_____

_____

_____

_____

_____

_____

_____

_____

_____

_____

_____

_____

_____

_____

_____

_____

_____

_____

_____

_____

_____

_____

_____

Personal HeartBeats

Personal HeartBeats

_____

_____

_____

_____

_____

_____

_____

_____

_____

_____

_____

_____

_____

_____

_____

_____

_____

_____

_____

_____

_____

_____

_____

_____

_____

_____

_____

_____

Personal HeartBeats

_____

_____

_____

_____

_____

_____

_____

_____

_____

_____

_____

_____

_____

_____

_____

_____

_____

_____

_____

_____

_____

_____

_____

_____

_____

_____

_____

Personal HeartBeats

Personal HeartBeats

_____

_____

_____

_____

_____

_____

_____

_____

_____

_____

_____

_____

_____

_____

_____

_____

_____

_____

_____

_____

_____

_____

_____

_____

_____